GHOSTS OF CINCINNATI

GHOSTS OF CINCINNATI

THE DARK SIDE OF THE QUEEN CITY

TERI CASPER AND DAN SMITH

HAUNTED AMERICA

Published by Haunted America
A Division of The History Press
Charleston, SC 29403
www.historypress.net

First published 2009
Second printing 2011
Third printing 2012

Manufactured in the United States

ISBN 978.1.59629.847.7

Library of Congress Cataloging-in-Publication Data

Casper, Teri.
Ghosts of Cincinnati : the dark side of the Queen City / Teri Casper and Dan Smith.
p. cm.
Includes bibliographical references.
ISBN 978-1-59629-847-7
1. Ghosts--Ohio--Cincinnati. I. Smith, Dan. II. Title.

BF1472.U6C3745 2009
133.109771'78--dc22
2009033687

CONTENTS

ACKNOWLEDGEMENTS

Many people have helped make this book possible. Before the project ever materialized, we saw a series of events brought about by several deceased family members who we think had a hand in making this book possible. Thank you to Debra Smith, our late stepmother. Your presence during this project was an amazing help. Thank you to the late Ernest Casper, whose help through life has been felt. A lot of pieces fell into place through much more than coincidence, so thank you to all who helped from beyond.

A special thanks to Kathy Casper, Michael Smith and Barbara and Jim Visota, our gracious parents who have nurtured our interest in the paranormal. Your openness and support of our ghost hunting adventures has instilled a deep respect within us for the unseen world around us. Whether skeptics or believers, many people freely gave their time and energy to help us in our quest to deliver the most complete and historically accurate account for each site.

Thank you especially to our precious girls Nevaeh and Fallon Smith, who we couldn't live without. You are very special to us, and you bring us so much joy and happiness. And finally, we couldn't ask for any better friends around us. Thank you for encouraging us every step of the way.

Thank you to the people and places who helped us dig up information about the unsavory past. With your help we were able to convey an important part of our city's history that usually goes untold.

INTRODUCTION

THE QUEEN CITY OF THE WEST

In 1788, a purchase of eight hundred acres along the Ohio River was made by Israel Ludlow, Matthias Denman and Robert Patterson. The men deemed the new town "Losantiville," a convoluted contraction meaning "the city opposite the mouth of the Licking River." To coax settlers into their town, they gave the first thirty who arrived four and a half acres of free land. Though the town had a slow start, settlers soon started migrating quickly.

One year later, the three founders authorized the construction of Fort Washington, which would stand to protect their citizens. Today a monument commemorates the fort near Fourth and Ludlow Streets. Three hundred soldiers moved into the fort to protect the city. The town would eventually take on the new name of "Cincinnati," in honor of a Roman citizen soldier, Cincinnatus, and also named in part for the Society of Cincinnati. Cincinnati was granted status as an incorporated city in 1819.

In the early 1800s, Cincinnati built a meatpacking center. This would bring great wealth to this city. Quickly this city would become home to the highest-grossing pork-processing plant in the United States. Farmers would bring their pigs to the processing center for cash. The meatpacking plant would then slaughter the animals, process the meat, package it and ship it out. The meat shipped out fairly easily since the state had recently built the Miami-Erie Canal, which ran through Ohio and into the South. The streets were littered with many pigs who escaped from private farmers, and the city soon became known as "Porkopolis." Townspeople ranted to the owner of the slaughterhouse that they did not want the pigs that were awaiting processing to get loose in the streets and add to the growing pig problem. The owner was very confident in saying that his pigs were secured in their pens and had no way of getting out. He assured them that pigs would fly before they escaped his establishment. One day thousands of the slaughterhouse pigs escaped and were running loose all over the city. The "Flying Pig" name stuck and is still widely used today. The city holds its annual "Flying Pig Marathon," and many comical flying pig statues are displayed around town.

The 1850s brought Cincinnati its first police force. The city also became home to the first full-time, paid fire department and was the first to use steam-powered fire engines. The high-class way to travel was by steamboats. The rivers were swollen with steamboats, with as many as eight thousand docking in the city each year. Author Harriet Beecher Stowe wrote a large portion of her novel *Uncle Tom's Cabin* while residing in Cincinnati. Her portrayal of African Americans enduring slavery caused debate during the civil rights movement. It later became the best-selling novel of the nineteenth century.

Ohio was an antislavery state in the early nineteenth century, and Cincinnati would often do its part to campaign against slavery. It would run newspaper articles to try to convince its southern neighbor of Kentucky to abolish slavery and set slaves free. The Underground Railroad helped smuggle slaves through Ohio, and Cincinnati was one of the last stops on the way to freedom. During the Civil War, the majority of Ohioans would fight for the Union. The government relied heavily on Cincinnati during this time. The city was a major supplier of new recruits and supplies for the war effort. It was also home to many soldiers and their families and was considered major headquarters for the Union.

The Roebling Suspension Bridge was built for travel by horse and buggy from Cincinnati to neighboring Kentucky and is still in use today. In 1869, the Cincinnati Red Stockings Association created the first professional baseball team in America, which would later be renamed the Cincinnati Reds after its founders. The Tyler Davidson Fountain was presented as a gift to the city in 1871 and is still the most iconic symbol of Cincinnati today. The statue sits at the center of the city on Fountain Square, with the genius of water atop the fountain.

By the turn of the twentieth century Cincinnati was the largest city in Ohio, and was the most densely populated city in the United States. The iron industry ruled Cincinnati, followed closely by meatpacking, cloth production and woodworking. The University of Cincinnati provided members of the community a proper education. Entertainment outlets included the art museum, Music Hall and Exposition Building, as well as many neighborhood saloons. Many major corporations have roots here and still maintain their headquarters here, including Kroger, Procter & Gamble, Cinergy, StarKist, Chiquita and many more.

Cincinnati faired better than most through the stock market crash and the Great Depression, mainly because of the river trade, though soon Cincinnati would have its share of hard times. In 1937, Cincinnati experienced a flood of epic proportions. The city was covered with eighty feet of water, and the only way to get around was by boat. It was estimated to have caused $20 million in damages and left one in eight people homeless.

During the next couple of decades, the city would spend time building entertainment centers, bars and nightclubs. Streetcars and inclines would give people a way to get around the city. The city would eventually give way to the ever-growing popularity of the motorized vehicle and would begin building roadways and major highways. The 1970s brought about another time of growth for the city. Riverfront Stadium was constructed and was the shared home to the Reds and the Bengals for three decades. In 2000, a new stadium was built for the Bengals and named after legend Paul Brown. The Reds received a new home with the completion of Great American Ballpark. The Cincinnati Riots of 2001 were the second largest riots in U.S. history. The riots were repercussion for the fatal shooting of an unarmed nineteen-year-old black male by a white police officer. The riots took place over four days of racial tensions.

Today Cincinnati is famous for its chili, with a signature dish being chili strewn on top of spaghetti, with beans, shredded cheddar and onions in a colossal mixture called a five-way. There are more chili parlors per capita here than any place in the world. It's also known for its Graeter's Ice Cream, LaRosa's Pizza and Montgomery Inn ribs. The city is home to many business headquarters, including about a dozen Fortune 500 companies. It's sometimes referred to as "the City of Seven Hills," on which it was built. These hills, combined with the dozens of parks, give the city some unforgettable views. Future plans for Cincinnati are very optimistic, with many large projects in the works to bring more promise to this ever-growing city.

The city has an unbelievable plethora of history to tell. There are some things that go unnoticed here when the sun sets on the beautiful hills. Cincinnati also has a dark history, with endless tales of tragedy. Tales of death and haunting plague this unknowing metropolitan area. We have gathered some of the most horrific events and tales of ghosts, separating fact from fiction. Each account is as historically accurate as possible to give you a better understanding of why the city is plagued with haunting activity. We invite you to sit back and uncover the dark side of the Queen City.

UNDERSTANDING GHOSTS

There is no scientific evidence that shows ghosts exist. We have heard this for years, but now it seems that the tables have turned. Many people now understand that something is happening in our environment that has not yet been fully explained. The statement today by many who are interested in this field is that there is no scientific evidence that shows ghosts *do not* exist. The word "ghost" is meant to refer to the spirit or soul of a deceased person. In popular culture, the word refers to a transparent being or an apparition. So why are dead people still hanging around? Surely they're not just waiting around for someone to scare, are they? The following is a guide to help you better understand the different types of ghosts, where they are found and why they stick around.

WHAT IS A GHOST?

Everything in the universe is made up of energy, including humans. At our most basic level, we are merely a pile of atoms. To give you an idea, a 150-pound person is made up of about one octillion atoms. That's a one followed by twenty-seven zeros, and that's a lot of energy. We know that we are made up of energy, and energy cannot be destroyed. Atoms create electromagnetic fields, which are believed by many to be the root source of paranormal activity.

The belief is that electromagnetic fields and energy can cause a disembodied spirit to exist in a semiphysical state. Although a physical person may not be present, his electromagnetic form can be. Some conditions can help produce ghostly phenomena. There are a few common conditions that are favorable for experiencing a ghost.

An atmosphere that is electrically charged or a nearby electrical source may give spirits the energy needed to manifest in several ways. Solar flares and solar wind can also cause changes in earth's magnetic field. Full and new moons can also cause changes in earth's magnetic fields and tides. Silent and dark areas are also conducive.

It is believed that ghosts can draw on heat energy in order to manifest, leaving cold spots behind. Haunting activity is most common during the overnight hours because of the lack of outside sources affecting energy. Light, sound and temperature can affect energy. When light and sound are limited and an energy source exists, the chance for a paranormal experience increases greatly. So it seems the old cliché of ghostly occurrences happening in the middle of the night and in the dark isn't so far-fetched.

TYPES OF MANIFESTATIONS

There are many forms of ghosts and paranormal phenomena. We will examine a few that appear in this book.

Intelligent Ghosts

This is the most understood and accepted form of ghost. Deceased humans will often make an appearance to friends, family members or strangers and are able to interact intelligently with the living. Intelligent ghosts can be familiar, such as deceased family members, or can be unknown to the viewer. They also carry their human essence with them by creating smells or sounds associated with them while they were alive. Because these ghosts seem to keep their personalities they had on earth, it is believed that they are still able to experience emotions. Some ghosts are friendly, loving and helpful while others are sad, depressed and angry. There are also the unknown intelligent ghosts. These are ghosts who are not readily identifiable to the viewer, such as a soldier or a former occupant of a home.

Full-Body Apparitions

This form of ghost is the most sought after and hardest to capture on film. It is believed that when a spirit gathers enough energy, it can manifest into a full head-to-toe ghost. Considering this theory, it is possible that a ghost may manifest only partially if it has limited energy resources on which to draw. These forms take on the characteristics of a human and can be identified by family or friends. When these apparitions appear in photographs, they can seem to be posing for a picture or can be totally oblivious to the camera. Some of these ghosts are seen in solid form holding conversations, which causes many people to mistake them for an actual person until they disappear in front of them.

Historically Familiar Ghosts

Ghosts who are historically familiar are readily identifiable as a well-known or famous person who is deceased, such as Abraham Lincoln. These familiar ghosts can exist in several different forms, ranging from a residual imprint to an intelligent haunting.

Residual Haunting or Imprint

These manifestations take on the appearance of a living human, but they seem oblivious to their surroundings. They repeat an event or sequence of events, as if on a loop that plays over and over again. Any attempts to interact with this type of manifestation are always met with the same unconcerned disposition, as if the viewer is the one who is invisible. The residual imprint remains the most commonly experienced form of paranormal phenomenon. Another theory is that these spirits may be unaware that they are being seen by the living and likewise are unable to perceive the living. They may be going about their daily routines just as the living do, walking through the same areas of a house or sitting in the same chairs. The main belief, however, is that these are not real spirits but rather an imprint imbedded onto the environment.

Poltergeist

The word "poltergeist" comes from the German word meaning "noisy ghost." These manifestations have considerable and sometimes dangerous power. This form of ghost is known for its ability to move or throw objects, make loud sounds such as knocking on walls and touching or pushing a person. In recent years, the idea of a poltergeist being a malicious ghost has been challenged. Poltergeist activity is normally centered around one person, usually a teenager. One theory is that large amounts of kinetic energy are released through telekinesis, causing a person to manifest poltergeist activity on their own. In essence, the person being haunted is the one causing the haunting without knowing it. This could explain why the activity seems to follow a person to different locations. Considering the number of stressed-out teenagers in the world, this phenomenon remains extremely rare. If a person can move objects with his mind, the idea of a ghost moving objects does not seem so strange. Many people, however, still hold the belief that poltergeist activity is an actual ghost that can affect its surroundings and not a person causing haunting activity with his own energy.

Nonhuman Ghosts

This type of ghost has intelligence, can interact with humans and can manifest emotions. They are very similar to an intelligent ghost but do not come from human origin. These ghosts have been referred to as entities or extracelestial. They have never had a human incarnation. Take a look at our world and all of its diversity in culture, race, religion and beliefs. If we apply this to the realm of ghosts, it is certainly possible that a human ghost may only make up a tiny percentage of spiritual beings in our universe. Nonhuman ghosts are rarely seen with the naked eye and are the hardest to document. Animals would fall into this variety of ghosts as well. Some seem to be angelic beings on a mission to help humans. Others are malevolent in nature, just as humans sometimes are on our planet. These dark and dangerous forms of nonhuman ghosts may account for what many religions call "demons."

Orbs

This type of energy appears in photos unexpectedly. They are also seen traveling at high rates of speed on film and sometimes change direction rapidly. One theory about these balls of light is that they are the most basic form of spirit energy in its earliest stage of manifestation. Other paranormal researchers write off orbs as dust or insects flying in front of the camera. This theory doesn't account for orbs that show up when no flash is used. It also doesn't explain why orbs usually show up at supposedly haunted sites and hardly ever in other photos. Orbs are still used by many researchers to gauge haunting activity but are weighed more heavily when accompanied by a high electromagnetic field or temperature drop.

Shadow People

This is a shadowlike supernatural being that has a humanoid shape but no distinct features. One theory is that these beings inhabit several dimensions, including the third dimension in which we exist. Mainstream science is fairly convinced that other dimensions exist and these creatures may come from one or more of them. Another theory is that they are the astral bodies of humans having an out-of-body experience. Some people report malevolent feelings in the presence of these beings, leading some to believe that they are demonic in nature.

Tulpas

A tulpa, also known as a "thoughtform," is a manifestation of mental energy. Something that is believed in by a mass collective consciousness becomes a physical manifestation in our dimension. Tulpas can sometimes take on their own images and behaviors. Good examples of other possible tulpas are Bigfoot and the Loch Ness Monster.

Bleed-through

The theory involving a bleed-through is that the past, present and future are all existing at the same time. If circumstances are right, there could be a rip in time whereby a past or future event could be witnessed. A bleed-through can occur in different settings, such as seeing soldiers on old battlefields or watching a doctor treat a patient in an old hospital.

Inanimate Objects

The strangest forms of ghosts and the most difficult to explain are those of inanimate objects such as ships, planes, cars and trains. Because these things do not have a consciousness, there is no good reason for them to appear in ghostly form. The most likely rationale is that they are a type of residual imprint, although they seem to occur far less frequently than those involving humanlike manifestations. Lighthouses have been known to shine a light after it has been removed, and school bells have been heard in abandoned schools.

WHY GHOSTS HAUNT

There are numerous reasons why ghosts haunt a location. At times they have no idea that they are dead. Death sometimes comes so fast that an individual may not realize he is dead. This is most common with murders, accidents or young children who are lost or confused. At times ghosts become attached to someone, someplace or something, refusing to let go of what they had in life. This could be a home they lived in or a place they loved. They can also be attached by feelings of guilt or regret. Some ghosts have unfinished business, and some are trying to complete a task. This could involve real estate, financial matters or simply the need to say goodbye to loved ones. Some ghosts want revenge. They are looking to bring justice to someone who has done them wrong. There are ghosts that have more altruistic motivations. In some instances, a ghost will appear to comfort a loved one or warn them of danger. Once its purpose is complete, the ghost will typically move on.

HAUNTING ACTIVITY SCALE

In order to give you a better sense of what kind of ghost or haunting activity is occurring in each story, a scale has been developed. This scale is based on our knowledge of haunting activity at each site. The Haunting Activity Scale will cover three main focuses for each chapter within this book. They are as follows:

FREQUENCY: how often sightings are occurring.
*Rarely; less than once a year
**Occasionally; once a year or more
***Frequently; multiple sightings each year

INTENSITY: how strong the haunting activity is.
*Minor; electromagnetic field readings, cold spots, feeling of presence
**Moderate; smells, orbs, apparitions
***Major; moving objects, intelligent voices, touching or physical harm

TYPE: what type of haunting activity is being experienced; for example: poltergeist, nonhuman or intelligent.

LOST AND FOUND

If tears could build a stairway,
And thoughts a memory lane,
I'd walk right up to heaven,
And bring you home again.
My heart's still active in sadness,
And secret tears still flow,
What it meant to lose you,
No one can ever know.
Since you'll never be forgotten,
I pledge to you today,
A hallowed place within my heart,
Is where you'll always stay.

—Anonymous

This is a tale of two eccentric soul mates whose time together on earth was all too brief. They longed to simply spend their lives together, but kismet would have other plans in mind. The passionate couple would only spend months as man and wife, but would spend eternity in each other's hearts. As Alfred Lord Tennyson says, "It's better to have loved and lost then never to have loved at all."

Elizabeth Boott was born in Boston in 1846, but everyone called her "Lizzie." When she was just a baby, her mother and brother passed away

The Cincinnati Art Museum in Eden Park is home to several unrested souls. *Authors' collection.*

from tuberculosis and left her father with the sole responsibility of raising her. Francis Boott and his daughter were much closer than most. He was completely devoted to his daughter and enjoyed spending all of his time with her. Francis was an artist, and little Lizzie wanted to grow up to be just like her father.

During her youth, Lizzie was very privileged. Her father was able to send her to the best schools and give her the finest of things. The duo lived as high-class citizens of Italy. They were prominent figures in their community and were very well liked. Little Lizzie was a polite girl and was quite the charmer. She grew up with fine arts and music all around her and took an interest at an early age. Francis nurtured her talents early on.

Francis would send Lizzie to exclusive art schools, with only an elite few joining in her classes. By her mid-twenties she was starting to be taken seriously as a painter. She was exhibiting her work on a regular basis and was following in her father's footsteps. She continuously craved new information and techniques, though never straying far from her father. They enjoyed traveling and learning together. This would eventually take them back to Boston, where they first heard of a fellow artisan by the name of Frank

A portrait of the late Frank Duveneck, who interacts with guests in Cincinnati Art Museum. *Authors' collection.*

Duveneck. They bought a painting from his exhibit but did not actually meet the painter for years to come.

Frank Duveneck came from less than humble beginnings. His mother was orphaned at a young age, and she and her sister were forced to walk barefoot to a neighboring town to find a place to live. She had to work as a servant girl in order to survive and lived the life of a peasant. Frank was born on October 9, 1848, as Frank Decker of Covington, Kentucky, just outside of Cincinnati. His father died during a cholera epidemic when he was only an infant. His mother remarried Joseph Duveneck later that year, and Frank was granted his last name, though Frank's birth certificate would still read Frank Decker. A bier garten was the family's main source of income, and they were considered to be very poor. He was of German ancestry and was known for speaking an entertaining mixture of broken English and German throughout his life.

While growing up, Frank's mother was a servant to a leading portraitist by the name of James Beard. This sparked Duveneck's excitement for artistry as a child. He would watch and learn from his idol and took great interest in his techniques. Frank practiced his skills in his youth and displayed a very advanced talent. He would paint signs and coaches when he was very young, and this would bring his family some much-needed income. When he was only fifteen, he began his formal training and started working at an altar-making shop, where he would decorate and paint murals for German churches. In 1869, Frank left the states at the age of twenty-one to study abroad in Munich at one of the leading art schools. Frank would call Munich his home for over ten years before meeting the love of his life.

Lizzie had heard that Mr. Duveneck would be teaching classes in Boston, and Lizzie jumped onboard with her father at her side. She fell for the professor of arts right away and often wrote to her friends of her secret love for Duveneck. Lizzie adored her teacher, who was two years her junior, and also respected his artwork. Eventually she spoke to Duveneck about him moving to Florence, where she and her father were living. This was to be a business venture, as she proposed, that would benefit them both. She would talk up this bright young painter to her rich friends and recommend that they buy his artwork, and she would get a commission for her services. She begged him to come back with her, and they could discover new art together. Florence promised him more beginnings and a prosperous future, and Duveneck didn't have much to lose.

In 1879, Duveneck found himself leaving Munich and heading to be with his former student Lizzie in Florence. Joining him for the move were more than a dozen of his friends and colleagues. It wasn't long after the move that Lizzie and Duveneck became romantically involved. The romance took off with a vengeance, and the couple soon discussed marriage. It appeared to be a natural decision for the new couple, as they just knew that they would only be happy in life if they were together.

This would not go over well with Lizzie's father, Francis. Francis did not trust the penniless Duveneck with his very well-to-do daughter. He feared that Duveneck was only after his daughter's money and had ill intentions for her. Francis's jealousy caused rage toward the new love interest, for he had always had Lizzie all to himself, and now this man was coming between the duo. Francis respected Duveneck as a painter but would still pressure Lizzie that he was no good for her. He made it very clear that Lizzie was not to have anything to do with this pauper. Francis managed to convince some of Lizzie's friends that her relationship was toxic, and they, too, would often advise of their disapprovals. This decision would weigh heavily on Lizzie's soft heart. She found it unimaginable to choose between the man with whom she had spent her entire life and the man with whom she wanted to spend her future.

Lizzie continued to struggle with the decision, with much pressure from both sides. She decided to get away from it all and head to Spain with some of her former classmates. This would give her some much needed time away from her father, whom she'd never been away from for any substantial amount of time. The vacation seasoned Lizzie's spirits and gave her a second breath of inspiration for her work. She came back determined to be successful and to make her own decisions in life.

Her escape when she returned was to devote herself to her paintings. She would take all of her frustrations out with her paintbrush. Every emotion burst out with a color on the canvas. Lizzie would spend her days slinging the paint, creating masterpiece after masterpiece. Quickly she would rise to the top, and she would become enthralled with her paintings. Many would start to talk about this beautiful and talented painter named Lizzie Boott.

In 1885, Lizzie and Duveneck announced their engagement. This came as devastating news to Mr. Boott, who felt that he needed to protect his daughter. Francis was frantic to guard his daughter's fortune. He had his lawyers prepare several documents before the marriage was allowed to take place. The first was an agreement that Duveneck would have no claim to Lizzie's fortune. The other transferred Lizzie's entire estate to Francis as sole trustee.

On March 25, 1886, Lizzie and Duveneck finally became husband and wife. They were married at the Bootts' apartment, and Lizzie wore a beautiful dark brown dress, which was the fashion at the time. The couple was so excited to finally have a chance to be together. They took off for a month-long honeymoon, where they could finally spend time enjoying each other's company, with no one else around.

Upon returning, the Duvenecks would spend all of their time together with big smiles that wouldn't wipe away from their cheeks. They were such passionate people, as many artists often are. They would use their time together painting and basking in each other's love. They would spend their days sharing their infatuation with each brush stroke, often painting the same things. No words needed to be spoken, for their love required no words.

They soon welcomed a baby boy into the world, named none other than Francis Boott Jr., and many things would change for the couple. The baby brought them even closer together and strengthened their bond. The joys of parenthood were felt by both Mr. and Mrs. Duveneck. Lizzie relished in motherhood and would divide her time with her artistry. One day Frank asked the mother of his child if he could paint her, so that he could remember his lovely wife just as she was at that moment in time, and Lizzie adoringly agreed. She wore her brown wedding dress, and he painted her in all of her glorious beauty. This was the happiest that the couple would ever be and the last time that he would ever paint his beautiful wife.

The baby was only a few months old in the winter of March 1888, exactly two years after the couple had finally celebrated their union, when Lizzie came down with a chill. Sadly, the lack of medical advancements at the time meant that the chill turned into pneumonia, and after just a few days Lizzie slipped into a cold and dark death. This came as sudden and unexpected news to everyone, especially to Duveneck. He couldn't grasp what had happened and quickly fell into a depression from which he would never recover.

Duveneck allowed Lizzie's father to have control over the baby's future. Francis decreed that his grandson would stay with his family in Massachusetts. Duveneck took jobs close to his son so that he could watch him grow. Francis had complete control over his grandson, much as he had with Lizzie. Duveneck was so distraught and depressed that he cared little about anything in his life. He spent his days after Lizzie's death creating a bronzed sculpture of her likeness, which has long been his most admired piece. The cryptlike sculpture depicts Lizzie lying peacefully with her hair pulled in curls on the side of her head, wearing a dress, arms folded across her chest and with a slight smile as she rests in peace. The memorial sits at her grave in the cemetery of the Laurels in Florence, Italy.

Duveneck maintained a primary residence in the Cincinnati area. He began teaching at the Cincinnati Art Museum and helped make it into what it is today. He was the dean at the Art Academy for some time. He found life to be very unfulfilling in the days without Lizzie. He seldom painted, and when he did it was with little emotion. He mourned for his wife every day. He began building a replica of Lizzie's original bronze monument to place on display in the Cincinnati Art Museum for his son to someday see. He sculpted Lizzie with every memory he had of touching her skin. The amazingly lifelike replica was placed in the art museum and is still there today. The museum has the largest collection of Duveneck's art and displays it on a rotating basis.

Duveneck passed away in 1919 at age seventy. Much of his artwork can be seen in the Cincinnati Wing of the Cincinnati Art Museum in Eden Park, along with his bronzed memorial of Lizzie. A portrait of her in her brown wedding dress is displayed on a rotating basis beside her bronzed memorial. It is said that the long-lost lovers have chosen this museum to meet in death. There have been many reports of a woman in a brown dress rising out of the monument and floating toward her lover's paintings and portraits, as if she was admiring his work. The ghost of Frank Duveneck has also been seen in the same room that they share. They have occasionally been seen darting through other galleries, admiring the art. Perhaps this is their secret meeting place now? Many guests and employees have admitted to seeing the woman in the brown wedding dress amongst the exhibits. Lizzie and Duveneck are forever surrounded by their passion for art and long to share it with us. One thing is for certain: they are finally in peace and will be together forever.

The art museum is filled with unique art and colors that brighten up the silent halls. The art speaks to you so powerfully that it feels like you have an obligation to only speak in soft whispers here. That is probably why Lizzie and Duveneck have been spotted hanging around so often. They aren't the only apparitions to be seen darting among the art. This museum has a few more unexpected guests that you may encounter.

If you follow the staircase up to the second floor of the art museum, it will take you to another room, filled with exquisite murals and unearthly occurrences. The walls of exhibit 204 are filled with twelfth- to sixteenth-century religious and Gothic art. The grand white pillars that encompass the white room lead you through a section of European art that celebrates religion. One of the paintings depicts angels and demons—a fitting omen for the gallery. In the center of the humbling room is a handcrafted Gothic-style bench, where patrons can rest and enjoy the most beautiful murals. The most capturing piece on display here is a massive altarpiece from the 1550s. With its wood frame and oversized opening doors, the former cathedral piece is hard to ignore. Thirteen panels are painted with eccentric colors, and each picture illustrates a scene from the Bible. This is the spot where people have reported seeing a levitating monk. The figure is dark and seems to be found near this altarpiece. Since the piece is about 460 years old, the monk could be from any time period. He probably would date back to about the same time period that the altarpiece would have been used in the church, making the monk roughly the same age. He has been seen around the altarpiece and can be seen encompassing the room. His presence is always abrupt and vanishes quickly.

Before leaving the art museum, make sure that you stop and see the 2,300-year-old mummy. There have been numerous reports of a seven-foot-tall

The art museum's mummy is said to be cursed. *Authors' collection.*

black specter that rises out of the mummy sarcophagus and bellows up through the ceiling. This is a rather rare specter that has no defined features, such as a face or hands, and is described more as a blur. People have reported uncontrollable nightmares after encountering the mummy. Guards have also reported a green glowing face staring at them and chasing them throughout the storage room, which is directly above the sarcophagus. The assumption is that the sarcophagus is the source of the storage room havoc, since it lies above the body.

Not much is known about this mummy, only that he was an adult male about thirty-five. He comes from Egypt, which has long been associated with mummies' curses, and disturbing them from their eternal resting spot seems to bring on a streak of bad luck. Often, after the bodies are disrupted, there are reports of large and eerie specters. With history on its side, these accounts could have some veracity. Some believe that the curses will not end until the mummies are laid to rest properly. Being on permanent display was probably not a person's ideal resting place. The constant tapping on glass and staring of visitors make for a pretty disturbing afterlife. The cycle of this curse may continue, and the mummy could become more aggressive as his patience wears thin. This mummy can be viewed just before the main exit on the first floor.

The Dark Side of the Queen City

Visiting the Cincinnati Art Museum is like traveling through time. As you browse through the galleries you find yourself engulfed in creativity and excellence. These walls speak to you and tell you of tales from centuries past. This elegance of the art mixed with the ghostly accounts give a whole new meaning to the saying "bringing art to life."

HAUNTING ACTIVITY SCALE
Frequency*
Intensity**
Type: residual imprint, shadow people, apparitions

MA GREENE

During the golden era of the steamboat, more than eleven thousand boats paddled their way across the Mississippi and Ohio Rivers. Today only a handful remains. The *Delta Queen* holds the distinction of being the only floating historic hotel in the United States. For many years, the steamboat has floated peacefully along the Mississippi and Ohio Rivers and through the heartland of the country. The ship, with its antique furnishings and crystal chandeliers, portrays a part of American culture lost in time. The *Delta Queen* has passed over two million miles of waterways and has entertained countless celebrities and presidents. Today a past captain of the ship stays with it, even in death. The captain keeps watch over the vessel and is not afraid to let it be known when she disapproves of something.

Work on building the ship's machinery began in 1924 in Dumbarton, Scotland, by William Denny & Bros. The cranks and paddlewheel shaft were created in Germany. At the time the *Delta Queen* was being built an identical vessel named the *Delta King* was built alongside it. Assembly took place at the Banner Island shipyard in Stockton, California, with both ships completed on May 20, 1927. The *Delta Queen* was ready for its maiden voyage.

The *Delta Queen* was put into regular service on June 1, 1927. It ran for the California Transportation Company of San Francisco along the Sacramento-San Joaquin River Delta, for which it was named. It was later acquired by the United States Navy in 1940 to transport navy reservists. In the fall of 1941, the ship was sold to be an excursion boat on the Hudson River on the east coast. The fate of the ship, however, would change on December 7, 1941, with the attack on Pearl Harbor. The ship was brought back into emergency service as a hospital transport for the navy. The boat eventually went to lay up with the Reserve Fleet at Suisan Bay, California, in 1946. It was purchased by Captain Tom R. Greene on December 17 of the same year. The boat was now property of Greene Line Steamers in Cincinnati. The ship was boarded up and transported by the tug *Osage* across the open sea. During its voyage, the ship became the only steamboat to ever pass through the Panama Canal. After twenty-nine days and more than 5,200 miles, the tug arrived in New Orleans with the unscathed steamboat. The *Delta King* was left behind and is now permanently moored in Sacramento as an operating hotel. After a major overhaul, the *Delta Queen* went back into service on June 21, 1948, under a new captain. Her name was Mary Becker Greene, affectionately referred to as "Ma."

Ma had always helped her husband Gordon with work around their ships from the time they founded Greene Line Steamers in 1890. She stood with her husband in the pilothouse, slowly learning how the operations of the boat worked. In 1897, she was the first woman ever licensed to pilot a steamboat in America. Greene Line Steamers enjoyed the reputation of being one of the countries most reliable steamboat companies. Ma was extremely well liked and respected for both her capabilities as a captain and her personality. Patrons boarded the ship specifically to enjoy Ma's company. She could cook, clean and entertain with the best, but she could also make repairs on the boat, keep the books and steer her way through the inland waterways that were thick with riverboats. She was tough, having given birth to her son Tom while stuck in an ice jam aboard the side-wheeler *Greenland*. When her son Tom bought the *Delta Queen*, she was the first one to move aboard and take up residence on the ship in cabin G. Ma was a fierce backer of the temperance movement. Although the ship had a bar, no alcohol was served. She was a member of a lady's social club, which looked down on drinking. She made it very clear that the sale or consumption of alcohol on her ships was strictly forbidden.

The boat paddled quietly over the water, with sounds of music filling its corridors and radiating to the shores it passed. During its peak of popularity, a five-night trip to Charleston, West Virginia, which included three meals a day, could be had for only eight dollars. The boat traveled to old American towns with old American names: St. Louis, Cincinnati, Louisville, New Orleans, Nashville, Memphis and Pittsburgh. Ma loved meeting and

The *Delta Queen* steamboat. *Courtesy Joe Schneid.*

interacting with her guests. By 1946, Ma was a widow nearing eighty years old. She continued to reside in her private stateroom aboard the ship. On April Fool's Day 1949, Ma boarded the *Delta Queen* for a routine trip to New Orleans. This would be her last voyage aboard the ship that she loved. On April 22, Mary Greene died in her cabin aboard the *Delta Queen*. She had piloted the finest steamboats for more than fifty-two years. After her death, the boat returned to Cincinnati and docked on the Ohio River. Ma Greene had spent fifty-nine years of her life in the steamboat industry, with fifty-two as a captain and pilot. She was one of the most beloved figures in the industry, and when she died a small piece of that romantic era died with her. Her son Tom died the following year of a heart attack while at the wheel of the *Delta Queen*.

Years passed, and eventually the ship was no longer owned by the Greene family. The ship changed hands several more times, including a sale to the Coca-Cola company. For years, the *Delta Queen* had been given special exemptions to continue operating as an overnight hotel because of its wooden hull. The last exemption ran out in October 2008. Supporters are still seeking an exemption from Congress that would enable it to once again travel the rivers as an overnight hotel.

Today, visitors and crew members report that Ma is still very much with the boat. An entertainer aboard the ship once saw a woman in a 1930s dress each night for three nights who seemed to disappear just as she looked up. She reported it to the ship's captain, and when passing a portrait of Captain Mary she exclaimed that the woman in the portrait was the same woman she had seen. When Ma isn't decked out in her finest, she roams the boat comfortably. Some guests have reported following a woman in a long green robe through the corridors only to have her disappear just as she turns a corner.

In 1982, First Mate Mike Williams was sleeping alone on the ship during annual repairs. He was awakened by an urgent-sounding whisper in his ear. He began hearing what sounded like a door slamming. Williams followed the sound to the engine room thinking that someone had boarded the ship. When he arrived, he discovered water pouring in from a broken intake pipe. The steamboat would have been in serious trouble if not for him being awakened by something—or someone.

During an overnight trip, Williams was contacted by a new employee who worked as a purser on the boat. She was worried about a guest, saying that an elderly woman called her to say she was feeling ill. She immediately went to seek out the help of Williams, who had medical training. Williams went

Mary "Ma" Greene and her husband Gordon. *Courtesy Franz Neumeier.*

to visit the stateroom and found it to be not only empty but also totally unoccupied. He returned to the purser, who had been frightened by the sight of an old woman staring at her through a window. Williams offered to walk the employee to her cabin. As they passed a painting of Captain Mary Greene, the purser became more frightened because the woman staring out of the painting was the same woman who had stared at her so disturbingly through the window. The two were later married and often tell people that Ma Greene introduced them.

On another occasion, a crew was on the boat filming a documentary. The cameraman was shooting footage in the Betty Blake Lounge. In the lounge were pictures of past owners of the ship, including Mary Greene. When the cameraman zoomed in on her picture, he screamed and fell back. Worried that their colleague had suffered a heart attack, other crew members rushed to his side. He could not speak but only pointed to the camera. Later, after regaining his composure, he said that as he focused on Mary Greene's picture, he realized that it was not a picture at all. He said that, while filming the picture, it had come to life! He refused to sleep in his cabin during the remainder of the trip.

Mary was strongly against alcohol, and it was for this reason that nobody dared to even bring up the subject while she was alive. Just after her death in 1949, construction began on a new saloon. Only days after opening the new saloon, a barge crashed into the *Delta Queen*, making a direct hit into the bar and destroying it. When crew members finally dislodged the barge from the steamboat, they were shocked at what they saw. The name on the barge was *Mary B.*

HAUNTING ACTIVITY SCALE
*Frequency**
*Intensity***
Type: apparition

THE WHITE ELEPHANT

Deep beneath the streets of Cincinnati is a series of tunnels and undergrounds stations of a subway that never once ran a fare. It took millions of dollars and an entire city of workers and supporters to build the now deemed "white elephant." Much of the remaining subway is buried underneath the streets, and portals lay hidden behind vines on the side of the highway. Today the barricaded doors lock in the secrets that the city would rather forget.

The Cincinnati Subway story begins at the Miami-Erie Canal, which ran through Ohio and directly through downtown Cincinnati. The canal was used primarily in the mid-nineteenth century to transport goods and people throughout the state. It was a very primitive form of travel and would take days or weeks to reach a destination. The canal was not maintained in a proper manner and soon brought bugs, disease and even death to the city. The water became incredibly polluted with the stench of dead animals and waste from buildings. In its wake, it brought a medley of different diseases, the worst of which was cholera. Cholera is spread through contaminated water consumption and often doesn't show any symptoms until hours before death. In 1849, the murky waters were blamed for causing over eight thousand cholera deaths in Cincinnati. This caused massive panic, and citizens would move as far away from the canal as possible. The canal was deemed unprofitable by 1856, and the city had officially abandoned it in 1877. City leaders would find an alternate use for the canal in later years, as it would become a major part of the Cincinnati Subway project.

In the late nineteenth century, Cincinnati started using streetcars as a mass transit system. It was a mere nickel to ride the electric cars, and it only took citizens about one hour to reach their destinations. This was the easiest and fastest way to get around the town. By the early twentieth century, the population grew, and Cincinnati became a booming town. Streetcars burst with people holding on to the railings for dear life. So many vehicles flooded the streets that accidents were a regular occurrence. Pedestrians found it nearly impossible to dart through traffic, and would often become casualties in the roadways. The streetcars started overcrowding the streets trying to keep up with demand. Private companies started offering a large horse-drawn carriage called an omnibus. It was ten cents to ride, but you could get around town much faster than in streetcars. The rough roads were difficult to maneuver in a horse and buggy. The terrain was very rugged and often threw passengers about the carriage. Cincinnati had to find an innovative way to deal with the traffic dilemma.

In 1884, the Cincinnati *Graphic* ran an article that it thought might bring new ideas for the city's traffic concerns. According to the *Graphic*, "The changes which time brings in all things cause many heartaches, but the heartaches of those who cling so fondly to the dead old ditch can in no degree compensate for the malarial headaches of hundreds who must suffer from its influences." On the cover of the publication was a large illustration of its proposal. It was a steam-powered train driving under the streets of Cincinnati through tunnels that would be built from the canal shell. By this time, the canal was filled with thick mud that hardly resembled water. It was a dried-up cesspool filled with disease and had become a breeding ground for mosquitoes. The canal trench was about forty feet wide and would bestow the city with a perfect jump-start for the subway project. This would save the city a lot of money and work from having to dig, as it already had a built-in pathway right through downtown. Though the proposal wouldn't be seen by the Ohio State legislature for almost thirty years, the *Graphic*'s proposal would continue to present the most logical way to deal with traffic problems.

In 1911, the city was finally granted the Miami-Erie Canal for use as a subway and to cover with a street. Morale was high for the new project. This would surely make the city's traffic problem disappear and would drastically cut travel time for commuters of the city. Businesses anticipated the potential of the subway bringing in new customers to their establishments, and help bring the city new life. Assurance that the city would have more visitors and increase population was what the subway had promised. This would make Cincinnati a booming town.

Looking up the Race Station stairs that were never used but are still maintained by the City of Cincinnati. *Courtesy Jake Mecklenborg.*

After assessing the subway project, the city came up with a $6 million price tag, after numerous cutbacks from the original $12 million. The bond was overwhelmingly passed in 1916, but the federal government had other plans in mind. America had been fighting in the First World War for two years, and funding for the war was very strict. Shortly after citizens approved the ballot, the U.S. government passed a bill that placed a hold on all bonds. Though the bond had been granted for the project, it could not be issued by law, so the subway once again had to wait its turn. When the war finally ended, all bonds were released for use. The problem was that during the war the cost of steel, labor and other materials had more than doubled in price. The cost of steel in 1915 was $55 per ton; in 1919 it has risen to over $105 per ton. The city sat with a $6 million check, and the new estimation of cost would be around $13 million. The city would go ahead with the project, knowing that there was no longer enough money for completion.

Construction on the tunnels finally began following the New Year's celebration in 1920. The city's new strategy was to build as much as it could with the money it had, which meant cutting back even more on the fifteen-mile beltway plan. The scheme then seemed to take on a dark and disturbing turn for the worst. When blasting the earth to make a path for the tunnels, no precautions were taken into consideration. People were living very close to the proposed subway path, and when the workers moved into those areas to blast, it caused great havoc. Inhabitants would be sitting in their homes comfortably when the blast would shake the earth and collapse the house on top of them. This became an all-too-often occurrence. Many houses were split in two, and foundations were ruptured. Citizens who were staunch supporters of the subway soon found themselves homeless because of it. It was reported that the subway collapsed and fatally injured several subway workers. Though the bodies of the workers have long been removed, their spirits still roam the empty halls today.

The project slowed as the money started to run out, and it was finally put on hold in 1925 until the city came up with a better plan. By this time this city was in disarray, and Cincinnatians were desperate to just forget the whole thing. The subway then sat abandoned, having accomplished only about 28 percent of its goal. By this time, only a two-mile tunnel through the canal trench, above-ground grading for seven miles, three short tunnels, many overpasses and a few under- and above-ground stations were completed.

The stock market crashed, the Great Depression followed, and the project received no attention for several years. There were many proposals to salvage what was already built and to cut out even more portions of the track to save money, but each one was overwhelmingly shot down by scorned citizens. The lonely subway lay dormant for years while proposal after proposal was turned down. By this time, cars were becoming more popular, so there wasn't the need for a subway. Personal vehicles had begun to take over roadways, and building and expanding roads had taken first priority. The bond debts would continue to accumulate interest. By the time they were finally paid off in 1966, a total debt of $13,019,982.45 was shelled out. The Cincinnati subway was constructed at the same time as the New York and Chicago subways. Their subways made them two of the busiest cities in America. The possibilities were endless for what the subway could have brought to this city. It was one of Cincinnati's biggest missed opportunities.

Today the subway is still considered a white elephant. As the years pass by, it is thought of infrequently and mentioned less often. People drive their cars by the remains daily, and most don't even notice it. Not much remains of the old project, though the city still maintains it. There have been a few proposals through the years for alternate uses such as a nuclear

One of the few portals still left standing. This is visible from I-75 near the Western Hills Viaduct. *Courtesy Jake Mecklenborg.*

bomb shelter, a wine cellar, monorail, shopping district and an aerospace testing facility—none of which panned out. The seven-mile stretch of above-ground grading was eventually demolished to make way for I-75. This left about two miles of tunnels that are currently located underneath Central Parkway, Hopple Street and Norwood, with the majority being located underneath Central Parkway. A few of the portals can still be seen from I-75 near the Western Hills Viaduct, though the doors have long been barricaded shut to keep out vandals.

These locked tunnels hold Cincinnati's secrets, one of which is the tale of the ghosts that haunt the halls. There are several spirits that have made their presence known underneath the earth, and they are believed to be workers who were killed by the collapsing tunnels. The atmosphere is thick and cold once you descend deep underground. There are no lights to find your path, and things are wildly thrown about by vandals. The halls are still and quiet. The smell is musty and dirty. The walls are damp, and the only sound is water drops hitting puddles. If it's not scary enough, the thought that ghosts encompass you throughout the darkness sends chills down your spine. Down here the feeling of being watched never goes away. It feels like the tunnels themselves weep with sorrow and a sense of death. Listen closely to hear the

The underground Brighton Station outbound platform. This dark tunnel leads to nowhere as spirits encompass you. *Courtesy Jake Meckenborg.*

cries and screams for help from the fallen workers as they grow louder and closer. With the lack of sight and sound, it's easy to feel a ghostly presence. Though access to the tunnels is limited, many people who have been down have reported feelings of being watched, followed and touched. The entities are doomed to spend eternity in these lonely tunnels and are desperate to leave their torment behind. They beg to be set free from their eternal prison. They sit and wait patiently to host their next visitors and plead with them to set them free. If you are lucky enough to get one of the rare chances to tour the tunnels, make sure you don't bring the workers home with you.

HAUNTING ACTIVITY SCALE
*Frequency**
*Intensity**
Type: residual imprint

CHECKING INN

The suburb of Lebanon is home to the oldest continuously operating hotel in the state of Ohio. It is the Golden Lamb Inn, a place from which some ghostly guests have never left. The Golden Lamb has more than one ghost, and with good reason. The inn has been operating since December 23, 1803, when a man named Jonas Seaman paid four dollars for a license to operate a "house of public entertainment." The establishment was named out of necessity. Many early pioneers were illiterate, so the business came to be known by the picture of the gold lamb on its sign. The lamb was recognizable and could be drawn rather easily.

More than two hundred years later, the site is home to several resident ghosts. It's not surprising given the long and colorful history that has taken place under the sign of the Golden Lamb. The inn has been known by many names throughout the years, including the Lebanon House, the Ownly Hotel, the Bradley House, Stubbs House and the Golden Lamb.

The original building stood roughly where the lobby and Dickens dining room stand today. It was a two-story building that became a well-known spot at which to rest, enjoy a good meal and meet others. Jonas Seaman's wife Martha was a great cook. With the help of several servants, the log tavern became known for great meals and clean and comfortable beds. On Main Street, stables were available to weary travelers and their horses. Pioneers sat around the hearth and shared stories of their own personal experiences of life in the wilderness.

The first courthouse in Lebanon was built directly across the street in 1805. Men of politics and law would meet at the inn, where they would enjoy corn bread, apple butter, venison and other popular fare. Politicians and lawmakers regularly discussed the goings-on of the newly formed state of Ohio. They also talked of plans for new roads and canals. In 1803, Jeremiah Morrow was elected as Ohio's first representative in Congress. A dinner was hosted in his honor at the Golden Lamb, where discussions began about building a road that would give access to other newly formed states. Representative Morrow introduced legislation that led to the construction of the National Road. The inn's popularity grew once again after the completion of the National Road. This was the first highway built entirely with federal funds. It opened the Midwest and the Ohio River Valley for settlement and commerce. The road still exists today as US-40, covering more than three thousand miles from Atlantic City, New Jersey, to San Francisco, California. The Golden Lamb was situated between Cincinnati and the National Road, and because of this, many prominent figures of the early 1800s found rest here.

As the area became settled, the cost of living increased dramatically. Having only paid four dollars for an operating license in 1803, Jonas Seaman paid ten dollars for the same license in 1805. His tavern was a bustling place of business by 1807, but still he faced rising costs. During that year, he placed an ad in the *Western Star*, asking those who owed him money to repay him immediately. His attempt was unsuccessful, and eventually he was forced to take out a mortgage and host a public sale in order to satisfy his own debts. It continued to be a popular place of business, but despite the apparent success of his establishment Jonas Seaman was forced to sell by his creditors. The new buyer was Ichabod Corwin, who originally owned the lots before selling them to Seaman. He built a brick hostel on the site in 1815 to replace the log tavern.

After Corwin opened the new brick building, he began hosting a wide array of entertainment. Circus acts pleased the crowds, and animal exhibits were held at the new establishment. Corwin stopped at nothing to entertain his patrons. He even hosted several "freak shows," featuring people with disabilities singing and dancing to amuse guests. With no stage or public place of entertainment, the Golden Lamb became the town's first theatre. The merriment and good reputation continue to this day.

Ohio Supreme Court justice Charles R. Sherman paid a visit to the Golden Lamb in 1829. During this trip, he died while staying at the hotel. He was only forty-one years old and left behind a wife and eleven children. As a result of Justice Sherman's death, his family was left with no means of supporting itself. Many of his eleven children were put up for adoption, including nine-year-old William Tecumseh Sherman. William was adopted by a Missouri politician and would later become a Civil War General, fighting epic battles and noting that "war is hell." Sherman has been seen strolling the hallways smoking cigars. The grief and guilt associated with Justice Sherman's untimely death may be keeping him at the hotel, forever looking for a way to reverse his death or perhaps looking for forgiveness.

Some claim that another man haunts the Golden Lamb. During the Civil War, a Congressman from Dayton, Ohio, named Clement Vallandigham was the leader of the Peace Democrats. This group, also known as the Copperheads, believed that the war with the South was unconstitutional and called for its immediate end. The group believed that the Confederacy had the right to secede from the Union. Although Vallandigham opposed slavery, he was also a staunch supporter of state's rights, saying that the government had no right to tell states that the practice was illegal. The Union loathed groups like the Copperheads, which were not helping the government win the war.

In April 1863, General Ambrose Burnside issued General Order Number 38. The order stated that "someone showing the habit of declaring sympathies for the enemy would not be tolerated by the Military District of Ohio." Shortly after the proclamation, Vallandigham made a public speech in Mount Vernon denouncing the war. He claimed that the Republican Party was attempting to further their quest for a dictatorship by ending slavery. He even went as far as to say that the war was being fought for the freedom of the blacks and the enslavement of the whites.

Just four days after his speech, Vallandigham was arrested at his home in the middle of the night for violating General Order Number 38. He was taken in his nightshirt and immediately transported to Cincinnati to face a military tribunal the following day. His arrest set off riots in the streets of Dayton. His supporters burned the offices of the *Dayton Journal*, and troops were brought in from Columbus and Cincinnati after martial law was declared. He was found guilty of aiding the Confederacy and sentenced to two years of confinement. President Lincoln feared an even more extreme backlash from Vallandigham's incarceration. More importantly, Lincoln did not want to create a martyr for the Copperheads. The president decided that he would commute the sentence and decided that Vallandigham would be banished from the Union. He was taken to

The Golden Lamb in 1936. *Courtesy Built in America Collection, Library of Congress.*

Tennessee, where he was escorted across enemy lines and handed over to the Confederacy. The Confederates didn't want him either, sending him to Canada. After the war ended, he was able to move about the country freely and returned to Ohio to practice law.

On June 16, 1871, Vallandigham was in Lebanon preparing to defend Thomas McGehan, a thug accused of murder during a barroom brawl. He was staying at the Golden Lamb, then known as the Lebanon House. His case rested on the idea that the victim Thomas Myers had shot himself accidentally. That evening, Vallandigham and two of his co-councils were near the Lebanon House conducting powder burn tests while firing a .32-caliber Smith & Wesson. They returned to the hotel at 9:00 p.m., and he was reminded that three rounds still remained in the revolver. On the way into the hotel, Vallandigham was handed another unloaded revolver that was to be used in the courtroom the following day. He went to his room and placed both revolvers on his dresser. He brought in his co-councils and began to demonstrate how Myers may have shot himself. He picked up the wrong revolver and slid it into his right pocket. He drew it out slowly, keeping the barrel pressed against his body, and snapped the hammer with his thumb. The revolver sounded a loud report through the hotel corridors.

According to his brother James, Vallandigham exclaimed, "My God, I've shot myself." Vallandigham leaned against a wall, wildly asserting that he had grabbed the wrong pistol. He tore open the clothing around his wound. Curious hotel guests soon began to gather around his room. At 9:30 p.m. he sent a telegram to his personal physician Dr. J.C. Reeve: "I shot myself by accident with a pistol in the bowels. I fear I am fatally injured. Come at once." Vallandigham was experiencing intense stomach pains and fierce bouts of vomiting.

Shortly after 1:00 a.m., Dr. Reeve and Vallandigham's sixteen-year-old son Charlie arrived from Dayton. Charlie sat by his father's side fanning the dying man. Vallandigham stroked his son's hair, telling him, "Be a good boy Charlie." Thomas McGehan was brought to his attorney's side. Witnesses said that McGehan sobbed uncontrollably. Vallandigham remained conscious through the administering of opiates and answered questions regularly. Despite his own physician telling him that he would die, his spirits were high. His fight continued through severe pain. At about 9:30 a.m., he experienced the most violent struggle yet. His skin tightened and his body shook violently as a grimace washed over his face. He then remained perfectly still for nearly fifteen minutes as his eyes became glossy. With startling movement, his body then stretched out upon the entire length of the bed. Taking a final breath, his head rolled back and forth as his eyes rolled away, leaving only the whites to be seen. The skin on his face tightened, his lower jaw dropped and a deep sigh escaped his throat. Vallandigham was dead at the age of fifty. Today, the room in which he shot himself is the Vallandigham dining room, complete with a stoic portrait of the man who now haunts the inn. Witnesses report Vallandigham's ghost as a thin man dressed in gray.

The ghost of a young girl is perhaps the most well-known ghost at the Golden Lamb today. On the fourth floor, you will find "Sarah's Room." Many believe the girl to be Sarah Stubbs, the daughter of Albert and Eunice Stubbs. The room named in her honor is a museum-like display consisting of old-fashioned dresses, dolls and toys. The display also includes some items that actually belonged to Sarah, including a rocking chair given to her by her aunt. When the items were moved from their original location in the Harriet Beecher Stowe Room, the little girl's ghost became very active. Sarah, however, grew up and eventually died of old age. For this reason, some people believe the ghost of the little girl is not Sarah. It may be that someone else has taken up residence among Sarah's belongings. Perhaps the room should bear the name of another young girl.

Politician Henry Clay was traveling with his family from Kentucky to Washington in 1825. Clay was the secretary of state for President John Quincy Adams. On July 11, his twelve-year-old daughter Eliza became ill with a fever while passing through Cincinnati. The family wrote it off as excitement for the trip. By the time they reached Lebanon, her condition had worsened. A doctor assessed the young girl, suggesting that she was too sick to travel. The family spent weeks in Lebanon waiting for Eliza to recover. Finally, the doctor affirmed that she would indeed make a full recovery, all but guaranteeing her father this assertion. Henry Clay then left Eliza and his family for Washington to resume his duties, but not without trepidation. He was just outside of the capital and had nearly completed his trip when he began reading the *National Intelligencer*. He was shocked by the news that met his eyes. His daughter Eliza was dead. Guilt and regret poured over Clay. He had deep feelings of remorse for leaving his family during such an emotionally trying time. His feelings were apparent in a letter to his wife Lucretia. According to the book *The Papers of Henry Clay*, his letter read, "I cannot describe to you my own distressed feelings, which have been greatly aggravated by a knowledge of what yours must have been, in the midst of strangers, and all your friends far away." Young Eliza was laid to rest in a cemetery near the inn. Her mother Lucretia

Sarah's Room, which holds some of Sarah's belongings. *Courtesy Greg Holmes.*

returned with her mourning family to their residence in Lexington. Many years later, the Clay family finally brought Eliza's remains home to the family plot in Kentucky. Many believe that the ghost of Eliza is one of the nonpaying guests at the Golden Lamb. Several patrons and employees have reported hearing noises from inside Sarah's room, which is locked and can only be viewed through Plexiglas. The little girl seems fond of the toys in the room, moving them around. Other guests have reported hearing the ghostly giggles of a young girl late into the night. It may be that both Sarah and Eliza are haunting the inn. They may pass time by playing together in the hallways.

According to records, as many as seventeen people have died at the Golden Lamb. Some reports of haunting activity are clichés like knocking on walls and hearing footsteps, while other occurrences are a bit more bizarre. One guest noted that he was very particular about leaving his slippers next to his bedside. While staying at the inn, he awoke during the night. He attempted to slide his feet into his slippers, only to find that they had been moved near the entryway, as if someone had worn them to the door before leaving the room.

Another tale tells of a homeless ghost. People have reported seeing a man dressed in rags walk into the inn and head upstairs to his room. This ghost may come from a time when a wealthy businessman once paid for an ill homeless man to stay at the inn. Despite the kind act, the man passed away during his stay. It seems the man has found a place he likes quite well at the Golden Lamb; it's possibly the only home that he ever had. On another occasion, a guest reported that someone tried to enter his room with a key about 1:00 a.m. He said that it happened again only a few hours later. This time the man arose from bed to see who was at the door. When he opened it, no one was there and the hall was silent. Employees have reported hearing doors open and close on the fourth floor inside of empty rooms.

De-De Bailey has worked at the Golden Lamb for thirty-two years. "This place is very unique. There's some kind of draw to the place that I can't explain. It is much more than an old building," says Bailey. She acknowledges that for the first twenty-seven years of her employment, she was the biggest skeptic about claims of the building being haunted. In February 2004, De-De was talking with the night auditor. The employee claimed that about 5:00 a.m. that morning she had heard a loud noise from a dining room upstairs. Upon investigating, several dozen glasses were found to have fallen off the shelves and cabinetry and were lying broken on the floor. Later that day during lunch, the Golden Lamb experienced a roof collapse, and a temporary roof was erected. As the day progressed, De-De was upstairs with some coworkers: "I took about ten or twenty steps away from the group, when I heard someone sigh right behind me." She turned around, expecting to see a coworker but instead found nobody. "That made the hair on my neck stand up," says De-De. What she heard may have been the sigh of a resident ghost who was equally stressed over the roof collapse. Because of the sequence of events that day, she says she now believes that something strange may be going on at the inn.

In 2009, the Golden Lamb celebrated seventy-five thousand days in business. The reputation of the inn and restaurant hasn't changed. Visitors can still enjoy a delicious meal or find rest in a clean and comfortable room. It was once said that if a person had the ability to sit in the lobby of the Golden Lamb without ever leaving, they would have witnessed the entire history of Ohio pass before their eyes.

HAUNTING ACTIVITY SCALE
*Frequency***
*Intensity****
Type: apparition, poltergeist, residual imprint, historically familiar ghost

THE GOVERNOR'S HOUR

Cincinnati's quaint suburb of Milford is home to a masterpiece of an Italianate-style home. The structure serves today as a museum dedicated to the Victorian lifestyle. Inside are examples of period art, furniture, china, clothing and photographs. The magnificent mansion was completed in 1867 by William McGrue. The home was referred to as "McGrue's Folly" at the time, because locals couldn't understand why he had built such a large home in the middle of nowhere. The building was a genius example of useful architecture. The home had a gas lighting system, a coal furnace that provided central heat and a gravity flow running water system. The home looks like a haunted mansion straight from Hollywood, and like a Hollywood movie, many sad and tragic events have taken place in the grand dwelling.

Promont was home to prominent Democratic politician John M. Pattison and his lovely wife Aletheia. They were the ones who would bestow the house with the Promont name. When he was only seventeen, Pattison enlisted for service in the Civil War at Camp Dennison. After the war ended, he attended Ohio Wesleyan University, graduating in 1869. His first public office was a seat in the Ohio House of Representatives. He later served in the U.S. Senate and the U.S. House of Representatives. Pattison's wife Aletheia died at Promont, leaving Pattison to raise their three children. He married Aletheia's sister Anna Williams after her death, and Anna helped him raise the children.

The Promont House in Milford. *Courtesy Ohio Division of Travel and Tourism.*

The Dark Side of the Queen City

In 1905, Democrats nominated Pattison as their candidate for governor. With his strong support for Prohibition, he gained many supporters during the campaign. Since the end of the Civil War, Republicans had held the office of governor for thirty-two out of forty years. Pattison ran an incredible campaign, gathering support from every corner of Ohio with his likeable personality. He created excitement for new policies such as an increased tax on saloons and railroad reform. He won the election and soon took his final office. During his inauguration as Ohio's forty-third governor, Pattison looked frail and felt ill. After delivering his inaugural address, he went to the Executive Chamber of the statehouse. For an hour, he rested with an overcoat draped on top of him. This one hour of rest was the only time he would ever spend in the statehouse. He watched the inaugural parade from behind glass so he would not be exposed to inclement weather. Afterward he was treated at Cincinnati's Christ Hospital, where he was found to be suffering from Bright's disease, or nephritis as it is known today. The governor's kidneys were failing, but he returned home to the warmth of Promont.

Pattison soon began experiencing dementia brought on by the disease. Waste products that are usually secreted into the urine were seeping out inside of him and poisoning his blood. He suffered through extreme bouts of back pain, vomiting and fever. At eight o'clock on the morning of June 18, 1906, two of Pattison's nurses noticed that he was not waking. An effort was immediately made to contact several doctors to aid the governor, but none was able to be found until two o'clock in the afternoon. By the time a doctor arrived, Pattison was nearly dead. He was experiencing edema, or swelling of the body. He was presumably in a coma, and his face was nearly unrecognizable. At 4:20 p.m., Pattison drew his last breath. He was only fifty-nine years old, leaving behind his wife Anna and three children. Lieutenant Governor Andrew L. Harris was immediately sworn in as governor following Pattison's death. The Republican Party had regained control of Ohio. Pattison's vision of reorganizing the state's institutions and various other projects would never be realized.

Almost immediately after he died, Pattison's deathbed began acting strangely. The bed would make noises and creaking sounds as if he were still rolling around in pain. The sheets would be made perfectly on the bed only to be rustled and out of place minutes later. This happened again each time the bed was made as if someone was still using it. The bed was eventually moved to another home in Batavia, Ohio, where the strange behavior continued. The family eventually had the bed stored away because nobody could get a good night's sleep on it. Pattison may still be suffering through his ailments, not knowing he has died. He may lie in this bed destined to continue his painful fight for all of eternity.

After the Pattison era, the home was the residence of millionaire tobacco farmer Henry Hodges. He grew enormous crops of tobacco and sold it at auctions. Tobacco auctions were a lively affair. Gentlemen showed up in suits and ties and wagered over the newly dried tobacco. According to legend, Hodges and his men had a tendency to leave tobacco stains in the house, which angered his wife. Both Hodges and his wife died inside Promont. If their ghosts are in the house, it may help explain a bizarre experience employees have reported. According to some claims, tobacco stains reappear on the floor immediately after being cleaned. The floors must be cleaned again of the tobacco-like residue. One theory is that the ghosts may be trying to use a spittoon that once sat where the stains occur. In any case, it is a rather gross form of haunting activity.

One night while working after hours, two employees inside the home heard footsteps coming up the steps. They yelled down that the museum was closed, but the footsteps persisted. When they approached the staircase to see who it was they found it empty. Having been quite frightened, the women ran out of the back door. Others report that footsteps from an unseen ghost can be heard upstairs when nobody is in that particular part of the house. The basement is especially active with strange sounds. People have reported hearing shuffling of feet and other sounds of movement in the basement. Some employees have refused to go into the basement at all. In the master bedroom, where Pattison died, people report cold spots that move around the room. Some have witnessed the bed move slightly, as if someone has just laid down on it. The museum has several different types of haunting activity occurring. With many period items, Promont may continue to be a familiar and welcoming home to the ghosts from its past.

HAUNTING ACTIVITY SCALE
Frequency**
Intensity**
Type: residual imprint, inanimate object

LADY IN GREEN

The Carew Tower stands tall near Fountain Square in downtown Cincinnati. At its base is the Hilton Netherland Plaza Hotel. Opened in 1931, the hotel is considered a French Art Deco masterpiece. The hotel was part of the first multiuse complex in the United States. In its original form, Carew Tower housed restaurants, a shopping complex, an automated garage, an office tower and a hotel. The atmosphere of the hotel today is that of unequalled elegance. Half an acre of rare Brazilian rosewood fills the lobby and mezzanine levels. Complete with an original Rockwood fountain and ceiling murals, the hotel beckons all who enter to retreat from their lives, if only for a moment, to enjoy the serenity it offers. The splendor of this place is matched by the elegance of the resident ghost. Hers is a story of love and tragedy.

Carew Tower was built to function as a "city within a city." Construction on the building began in September 1929, just one month prior to the stock market crash that would lead to the Great Depression. After the stock market crashed on October 24, 1929, the intricate details of the plans for the building were amended. The grand architectural motifs and decorative metals were only added to the building up to the third floor, while all floors above the third were built with plain bricks. The entire building took only one year to complete.

Because of the speed at which crews worked, there were some accidents. One accident involved a painter who was working in the main lobby, which is now the Palm Court. While working the painter fell to his death, leaving

The Palm Court inside the Hilton Netherland Plaza. *Courtesy John Wright.*

Carew Tower, with the Hilton Netherland Plaza Hotel at its base. *Courtesy Michael Walton.*

behind a distressed widow. Legend says that the man's widow checked into the hotel after the grand opening and promptly threw herself out of a window. Many have seen the ghost of the Lady in Green throughout the hotel.

The Lady in Green is an African American woman who is always seen wearing a formal green ballroom dress. One day an employee entered an elevator with a woman in a green dress. The two talked about how beautiful the Hall of Mirrors was. The man turned just for a second, and when he looked back, she had vanished. One night another guest came to the front desk frantic, wearing only his underwear, saying that he was checking out. Something startled him so badly he wouldn't return to the room for proper clothes or his belongings. On another occasion, a guest came shooting out of an elevator. He said that he had seen a woman in a green dress on the elevator with him and that she had disappeared.

There have been several reports of disembodied voices as well. A voice has been heard asking for help when no person can be seen. This scared one employee so badly that he quit immediately. According to some accounts, a person was once tapped on the shoulder and asked for help by the same invisible woman. The Lady in Green has also been seen on the mezzanine level near its decorative murals. During renovations in 1983, several construction workers claimed to have seen the lady. The Lady in Green has also been seen in the Hall of Mirrors, a grand ballroom with many chances to see a ghost. While walking through the room, you are met with glimpses of your own reflection out of the corner of your eye. In some cases, guests who have used the Hall of Mirrors have seen an extra guest that is not on the guest list. As always, it is a woman in a green dress, walking the room with an almost curious demeanor.

Her ghost may be searching the hotel for her husband who was killed. This may be why she is asking people for help. Whatever her reasons for haunting the hotel may be, she never appears to be trying to cause any problems. The Lady in Green seems content here among the finely crafted pillars and elegant décor. If you visit the ornately decorated hotel, perhaps you will catch a glimpse of the famous resident ghost.

HAUNTING ACTIVITY SCALE
Frequency*
Intensity***
Type: apparition, intelligent ghost

THE MIDNIGHT TRAIN

The Cincinnati Museum Center at Union Terminal hosts hundreds of tourists every day. It is a very recognizable building with great grandeur. Many people visit this family-friendly place, but few know that this building is haunted. At night when the doors are locked, security guards patrol the empty hallways of the former railway, but they don't keep watch alone. This majestic building is closely guarded by the afterlife.

In the late 1800s, the fastest and most convenient way to travel between cities was by passenger train. In this era, cities that did not have a rail line were left in the dust of the modern world. The city of Cincinnati was becoming a booming town mostly because of the many rail lines that connected throughout the city. The rail cars brought more than just goods to this great city. They brought prosperity, growth and new citizens aboard each car.

There were seven rail companies in Cincinnati: the Baltimore and Ohio (B&O), the Chesapeake and Ohio (C&O), the Cleveland Cincinnati Chicago and St. Louis (CCC&StL), Louisville and Nashville (L&N), Norfolk and Western (N&W), Pennsylvania and Southern lines. These seven rail lines all ran train cars out of five different rail stations dispersed throughout the city, and it was quite chaotic. This made it hard on passengers who had to transfer trains at other stations since they were responsible for securing their own transportation in between rail stations before their departure.

In the 1890s, the City of Cincinnati decided that it was time to create a uniform train station for all seven rail lines. This would make transportation a much easier transition in and out of the city. It wasn't until 1928 that construction would begin on the Union Terminal project. The city had passed a bond for the project with a giant price tag of $41.5 million and had very high hopes for the prosperity it would bring Cincinnati. There was very close attention paid to every aspect and detail of the golden building. The city hired top architects Alfred T. Fellheimer, Steward Wagner, Paul Philippe Cret and Roland Wank to design the largest half dome building in existence. German artist Winold Reiss was brought in to design the giant mosaic murals that still run along the walls of Union Terminal, though some of the murals were relocated to the Cincinnati/Northern Kentucky Airport in the 1970s. The unique structure lies on 287 acres and has ninety-four miles of tracks. This was one of the largest projects that the city had ever taken on and took five years to complete.

On March 31, 1933, Cincinnati's Union Terminal had its dedication ceremonies and opened for business. Unfortunately, as soon as the doors were open, it seemed the business encountered more problems than it would have imagined; the project was destined to fail. The 1930s were a time of decline for traveling by train, and Union Terminal was no different. The stock market crash and the Great Depression were mostly to blame. The rail yard was used less and less throughout the years. By the late 1930s, it had already become referred to as a "white elephant," with train travel slowing and nearly stopping.

The terminal gasped for a breath of life through the early 1940s, when it finally found its opportunity to rise again. America had involved itself in the Second World War, and the cheapest way to ship newly enlisted soldiers was by train. Train cars loaded up as many as twenty thousand soldiers per day, and the train whistles sounded off in triumph. The railroad was pushing out cars as fast as it could drive them in. Cincinnati became a major transport point for soldiers during the war.

As quickly as it found its new life, though, it faded away. After the war ended, there just wasn't the need for trains. Cars had become a popular commodity, and people found better ways to travel than by train. It looked like a bleak future for the railway. Business for the terminal continued to wither away through another decade. In 1958, the last passenger train pulled out of the terminal. Cargo trains continued to run until October 28, 1972, when the last train car left the abandoned station. In an effort to save the train station from total demolishment, the city declared it a historic landmark. During development projects a lot of the original structure and artwork were damaged or moved.

Winold Reiss was hired to paint the beautiful artistry inside Union Terminal. *Courtesy Built in America Collection, Library of Congress.*

The station sat empty for quite a few years until it was eventually developed into the Land of Oz, a classy shopping mall. Vendors leased storefronts inside the terminal and sold clothes, shoes, food and souvenirs. The plan was never really successful and only lasted a few years, though some vendors would stay behind and use it as a flea market for several more years. There were high hopes for restoring the building and bringing it new life.

In 1986, Cincinnatians decided to give the old Union Terminal a new purpose. Voters passed a $33 million bond issue to restore the building, and turn it into what is now the Cincinnati Museum Center. The project also received another $11 million to help with the restoration project from the City of Cincinnati, the State of Ohio and from private funding.

The Cincinnati Museum Center at Union Terminal finally opened in 1990. It is host to several different museums and special exhibits. The Museum of Natural History will guide you through all things nature. The Cincinnati History Museum has the largest World War II homefront exhibit in the nation. The Robert D. Linder Family Omnimax Theatre plays hourly special features. The dome theatre is five stories high and seventy-two feet in diameter. This is one of the most successful Omnimax theaters in the world. The Cincinnati Historical Society Museum and Library has one of the most significant regional history collections in America. The year 1991 saw the

Union Terminal train station is now the Cincinnati Museum Center. *Courtesy Built in America Collection, Library of Congress.*

A phantom pilot takes flight at night in this World War II replica plane at the Cincinnati Museum Center at Union Terminal. *Authors' collection.*

grand return of the passenger trains, when Amtrak established a schedule for the Museum Center. Soon to follow was the opening of the Duke Energy Children's Museum in 1998. The Children's Museum brought in over 450,000 visitors in its first year. Since it opened, it has been consistently ranked in the top ten children's museums in the world.

The museum center has had great success since opening up in 1990 and continues to promise more. People now constantly flow through the once empty hallways of the former major railway. Millions of people have visited the Cincinnati Museum Center over the years, and some of the guests have decided to stay forever. The Cincinnati History Museum, known for its World War II exhibit, has spent great time and energy to gather as many relics from the war as possible. One notable piece is the World War II replica plane that hangs high above the front entrance of the museum. This aircraft cannot even fly, but a seat is still left open for its lonely ghost pilot. A young World War II soldier appears to pilot the plane in full uniform consistently in the evenings. Night guards see this pilot on a regular basis. Visitors have often been known to catch a glimpse of the lost soldier. It's rather mysterious why the soldier has taken up residence in a replica plane, but it might be his way of trying to find his way home. This may have been his last stop before being shipped off to his death in World War II.

Union Terminal was at its prime during the Second World War. In back of the old rail yard, cries of joy and the welcoming back of soldiers can be heard. There don't seem to be any actual ghosts here. Instead, the event had such an emotional impact that it is imprinted on the environment and is destined to repeat forever. The soldiers and families would have been so desperate to see their loved ones again that it was just emotional chaos, and those moments of joy led to the reoccurrence as a residual haunting today.

Another paranormal phenomenon involves a woman named Shirley. Legend has it that she was a dedicated night guard in the early 1990s who was hired to catch a ring of thieves that had been stealing computers at the newly opened Museum Center. Shirley was the only one to catch the thieves in action. She caught up with them on the fourth floor, a struggle ensued and the thieves subsequently shot and killed her. She has sworn to protect the halls even in her death. Her footsteps can be heard as she patrols the halls. She will close and lock doors behind her, as if securing the building. Flashlights have been seen making the rounds through the corridors where the halls are empty. Shirley takes her job very seriously and is still the museum's most dedicated worker. Her job now is to keep this old train station safe for all of the visitors.

Since its completion in 1933, this old building has endured a lot. Not only does it have some great ghost stories, but it also has become a landmark of Cincinnati. The half-dome building is one of the most recognizable places in this city. The knowledge and hands-on activities that you can learn here are endless, and there is no doubt that you will leave the Cincinnati Museum Center with a smile on your face and memories for a lifetime.

HAUNTING ACTIVITY SCALE
*Frequency***
*Intensity***
Type: residual imprint, apparition

WHAT LIES BENEATH

Spring Grove Cemetery was established in 1845, and today is the second-largest cemetery in the United States, with Arlington National Cemetery being the largest. It was originally established in response to a cholera epidemic. Cemeteries often became overcrowded and unkempt trying to keep up with casualties from the deadly outbreak. The city needed more land on which to build. They chose a peaceful parcel of land where people could mourn the loss of their loved ones in a beautiful setting.

Spring Grove Cemetery covers 733 sprawling acres, of which only 400 are used and maintained today, ensuring that the cemetery will be used for hundreds of years to come. The plush grass is scattered with huge Gothic monuments that exhibit intense attention to detail. In 1987, the name was changed to Spring Grove Cemetery and Arboretum to incorporate the collection of prized plants and trees. This land provides extraordinary views that you won't find anywhere else. It is the perfect place to take a serene walk—and to have a firsthand encounter with death.

Among these four hundred carefully landscaped acres are twelve peaceful ponds, hundreds of beautiful trees and endless pieces of architecture to admire. The array of horticulture paints an amazing landscape portrait. Trees, bushes and flowers have been handpicked and shipped from all over the world to be planted in the rich soils of Spring Grove. To truly appreciate the pure beauty of this place you must plan an afternoon. There are many walking trails filled with serene silence. This does not feel like a place of sorrow, but rather a royal residence where the deceased eternally rest in peace.

There are three chapels among the Spring Grove acres: White Pine, Cedars of Lebanon and Norman. The latter has quite a unique history and has several reports of strange occurrences. Norman Chapel was built in 1880 from limestone and sandstone, which lends a sandlike appearance to the structure. The interior is filled with majestic arches, stained glass and bronze doors. Today it is used for a far different reason than its original intended purpose. The plan for this noble chapel was to construct a crypt below the first floor, but it was never finished. The cemetery used this basement from 1881 through the early twentieth century as a jail. It was used to incarcerate those who were caught speeding through the cemetery in their horse and buggies. If you go to the western side of the building, you can see the windows still have the jail bars intact. At one time, three night guards would stand post here and were ordered to shoot trespassers unless they immediately identified themselves. Cameras have captured many orbs here, and it has been said that you can sometimes hear eerie cries from those who were incarcerated here.

There are many glorious mausoleums scattered throughout the grounds. Each mausoleum is uniquely decorated with high ceilings, stained glass, bronzed doorways and sometimes even prized possessions. Dexter Mausoleum was constructed out of sandstone by James Wilson between 1865 and 1869. Sandstone is known to be a very weak building material, and despite numerous attempts to restore it, the memorial, too, will soon share the same fate as its inhabitants, who are gone forever. The monument stands on a lot that overlooks Geyser Lake and Strauch Island. People have reported that from the porch one can sometimes see the spirits of two pure white wolves passing by the lake. These lupine apparitions will stop and stare at intruders with glowing green eyes, as if wondering what you are doing, and then will vanish. They often roam this land and will guard it from vandals.

In the late 1800s through the 1900s, many of Cincinnati's finest citizens were buried in the cemetery and have provided some very interesting memorials. It is the final resting place of many soldiers, including 999 plots for Civil War soldiers. There are also 41 Civil War generals interred throughout the grounds, including the rather infamous General Joseph Hooker. "Fighting Joe Hooker" was best known for his stunning defeat by General Robert E. Lee. Hooker was also known for keeping his men's spirits up by having lots of ladies of questionable virtue come to camp to take care of his men. They became known as "Hooker's Women" and eventually just "hookers." Another Civil War plot belongs to the

A picture of Norman Chapel in Spring Grove Cemetery. The basement served as a jail for people driving carriages too fast. *Authors' collection.*

McCook family, who had eight sons who fought for the Union. They have a spectacular memorial and family plot where many of the sons are laid to rest. There are also around 33 soldiers buried here from the Revolutionary War, as well as many other wars.

There are many notable political figures who are inearthed here. Ten governors from three different states, as well as U.S. representatives and senators, are buried at Spring Grove. Nicholas Longworth represented Ohio's first district in Congress and was the Speaker of the House in the early 1900s. Judge Jacob Burnet was the author of Ohio's constitution. Salmon Chase served as Ohio's senator, governor, secretary of the treasury under Abraham Lincoln and chief justice of the Supreme Court. He also helped establish Spring Grove Cemetery, and someday you may find yourself lucky enough to check him out on the rare $10,000 bill.

Some of the beautiful monuments belong to Cincinnatians whose names are branded in modern society. Bernard Kroger established the ever popular chain of grocery stores that bears his last name, which has become the largest chain of supermarkets in America. Stephen Gerrard gave us the honeydew melon and the Elberta peach. One of the most recognizable duos in the cemetery is William Proctor and James Gamble, who founded the

A headstone of the late C.C. Breuer in Spring Grove Cemetery. The lifelike bust is said to contain his real eyes. *Authors' collection.*

Proctor and Gamble Corporation. Though the two passed away long ago, the corporation still has its headquarters in Cincinnati and is one of the largest brands of household products in the world.

You will find the atmosphere in Lot 100 of Spring Grove peaceful and serene, but there is one monument in particular that will capture your attention. It is the grave of C.C. Breuer or "Charles." There is little information left to be found about Charles, but the lore remains the same. Charles was born in 1845 and passed away in 1908. The legend says that he was an optometrist throughout his life and became extremely obsessed with eyes. In his will he decreed that his real eyes be removed from his body, encased in glass, and then placed inside his bronze bust so that he may watch over his grave. His bronze statue towers over those who visit, and his bust has a very lifelike appearance to it. Some horrified guests have reported that the statue's eyes dilate and follow the path of the viewer. Some have reported that his entire bust can move around the monument and can even speak to you if he is disturbed. Rain seems to enhance the features and creepiness of the statue. He waits and guards his grave and will protect it from any trespassers.

Spring Grove representatives will tell you that people buried here seem rather happy to have this as their final resting place and that the spirits do not act out here. To be buried in the quaint peacefulness of the grounds here is an honor indeed. The spirits here seem happy to be remembered in such a caring way. There are no reports of violent spirits—only those who will protect the cemetery and its inhabitants. If you find yourself feeling like you are being watched or you feel a gentle touch on your shoulder, then you should welcome the curious spirits, as they are only there to watch over you. Cemeteries are not usually where a spirit would want to spend a lifetime, but an eternity at Spring Grove wouldn't be so bad.

HAUNTING ACTIVITY SCALE
Frequency*
Intensity**
Type: apparition, inanimate object

ANNIE'S ART

On the extreme eastern edge of downtown Cincinnati lies a building with a past as grand as its architectural perfection. It is the Taft Museum of Art, and it has a long and colorful history, including a few resident ghosts. This has been the former residence of some of the most prominent names in Cincinnati's history.

In 1812, a nine-acre plot of land on Pike Street was purchased by Martin Baum. He was twice the mayor of Cincinnati and is credited with founding the nation's first public library. Baum made his fortune through several enterprises, including real estate, a sugar refinery and the steamboat industry. He had a home built on the site that was completed in 1820. Today, it stands as the oldest surviving wooden structure in the city and is one of the finest examples of Palladian-style Federal architecture in the country. Baum was directly affected by the Panic of 1819, an economic downturn that saw bank failures, foreclosures and widespread unemployment. By 1825, he was forced to sign the deed for his home back to the Bank of the United States.

The home was purchased by Nicholas Longworth, a prominent politician who held several offices, including Speaker of the House for the United States House of Representatives. He redecorated the interior of the home extensively and named it Belmont. Landscape murals still exist in the foyer from the time when he lived in the house. Longworth hired Robert S. Duncan to paint the murals. They stand today as one of the finest suite of domestic murals ever painted prior to the Civil War.

The Taft Museum of Art in 1940. *Courtesy Built in America Collection, Library of Congress.*

Industrialist David Sinton bought the home in 1871. He was in the iron business and owned two iron furnaces, which put out as much as five hundred tons a year. Sinton would produce the iron at ten dollars per ton and would sell it for eighteen. When the Civil War began, Sinton had seven thousand tons of pig iron stockpiled. Suddenly, the demand for iron pushed its market value through the roof. Sinton sold his iron for seventy-five dollars per ton as he raked in enormous profits. Through all of his success, Sinton was always known as a penny pincher. His frugality was apparent to all who met him. After purchasing the home on Pike Street, he was able to walk to his office. On his walk he passed his favorite saloon, at which he would order a double shot of whiskey each morning. A double shot was cheaper than two individual shots, so he would take half of his drink in the morning and the other half on his way home in the evening. He was also known to order a headless beer. The beer would be filled to the top so the foaming head wasn't taking up so much space. Some bars in Cincinnati offer some version of a "Davey Sinton" today. Sinton continued to build his fortune with the elegant Sinton Hotel in downtown Cincinnati. When he died in the home in 1900, he was the richest man in Ohio, leaving $20 million to his daughter Annie.

Sinton's daughter Annie had lived in the home with her husband Charles since 1873. Upon Sinton's death, Annie inherited the home. Charles was the half-brother of President William Howard Taft. In 1908, William Taft stood on the steps of the home as he graciously accepted his party's nomination for president. Charles worked as an editor for the *Cincinnati Times-Star*, later known as the *Cincinnati Post*. The Tafts followed in the footsteps of the Lytle family as the most prestigious and elegant family in the city. Annie and Charles found it important to begin a collection of porcelains, old paintings and decorative European arts so the community was able to study the fine arts. When Charles died in 1929, Annie made a $2 million donation to the University of Cincinnati as a memorial fund in her husband's name. In 2005, the fund was transformed into the Charles Phelps Taft Research Center. Annie Taft died in 1931, leaving the historic home and the entire private art collection to the people of Cincinnati. It has operated as the Taft Museum of Art since 1932. Ultimately, their hope was that Cincinnatians would be able to apply a fine arts background in their own lives and in their jobs. The collection consists of 690 of the finest pieces the Tafts could gather. The most important piece is an ivory virgin from Paris that dates back to about 1280. According to the Louvre in Paris, it is the single most important Gothic sculpture in the world.

Anna Sinton Taft, who is said to haunt her former home. *Courtesy Don Prout.*

Being as old as it is, the home is treated as part of the art collection. The museum faces all of the problems associated with an old wooden home but continues to be maintained in an elegant manner despite this fact. Installed in a domestic setting, the collection is reminiscent of a time when citizens were enlightened with a sense of courtesy toward one another that is not commonly found in today's society.

Many people claim to have seen Annie's ghost in and around her former home. One afternoon during a concert in the backyard garden a security guard was surprised by what he saw on a second-floor balcony, which was inaccessible to the public. He radioed up to the guard on that level, who looked out on a beautiful woman in a pink dress tapping her foot to the music. It was Annie who was enjoying an afternoon of music in the garden. Employees have arrived in the morning to find that one of the gallery rooms is locked shut from the inside by a chair being placed under the doorknob.

Several visitors to the museum have reported being tapped on the shoulder by an unseen presence. In the gift shop, books have been known to fly off the shelves for no apparent reason. Some guests have reported seeing an apparition of David Sinton inside the house. While waiting to pick up a security guard, a person claimed that someone was standing inside the home waving out the window. When telling the guard about seeing them wave, the guard replied that no one was in that part of the house as it was under alarm. According to staff, the ghosts seem especially active during the times when exhibits are changed. With such a beautiful home and collection of art, it seems that several former residents aren't quite ready to leave.

During our visits to the Taft, we have come in contact with a curious ghost visiting us near the gates on numerous occasions. We have experienced cold spots and high electromagnetic field readings that are accompanied with photographs of orbs and mists. It seems that someone has stayed behind to look over their beloved home. With a rotating display from the Taft's personal art collection, perhaps Annie and others come here to find solace through the art they so loved.

HAUNTING ACTIVITY SCALE
Frequency ***
Intensity ***
Type: apparitions, intelligent ghost, poltergeist, historically familiar ghost

THE BLACK WIDOW

Love, tragedy, betrayal and retribution. Throw these things together, mix in millions of dollars and you have the perfect recipe for a ghost. Eden Park is known for its serene settings and panoramic views. It is an oasis for many looking to get away from everyday life. When the sun sets on this picturesque landscape, a much more sinister side is revealed. A ghost with a very unique story wanders these grounds looking for a peace that she may never find.

The dark and nearly unbelievable tale comes from a time when Cincinnati was at the peak of its golden era amid the 1920s. During Prohibition speakeasies flourished and bootleggers made millions. The story of one whiskey peddler in particular exemplifies the power that alcohol carried during the Prohibition era.

George Remus came from humble beginnings in Germany and would rise to be one of the most successful and powerful bootleggers this country has ever seen. George's father, Franck Remus, came from Freideberg, Germany, near Berlin. Franck was an apprentice in a woolen mill and eventually married the mill owner's daughter, Maria Karg, in 1871. They had three girls who all died in infancy. George Remus, their fourth child, was the only child who lived. When George was four and a half years old, he departed Germany with his parents for Milwaukee, Wisconsin, where several other members of the Karg family had previously settled.

After arriving in America, tragedy continued to strike the Remus family. The family fell on hard times almost immediately after settling in Milwaukee.

George Remus, "King of the Bootleggers." *Courtesy Jack Doll Collection, Delhi Historical Society.*

Frank, who dropped the Germanic spelling of his first name after arriving in America, was no longer a weaver, but instead had been doing work as a lumber scorer. He became crippled with articular rheumatism and was no longer able to work. The family left for Chicago, where George would become the main provider for the family by his early teens. An uncle, George Karg, ran a drugstore in Chicago, and young George Remus left school to work as his assistant.

According to everyone who knew George, he was a good and responsible young man. He loved books, had a great sense of humor and seldom had to be scolded. He became a strong swimmer and a well-known member of the Illinois Athletic Club's water polo team. He was confirmed in the Lutheran Church, despite the fact that neither he nor his family was very religious. As he grew older, he was sufficiently curious enough about different churches to attend Catholic, Christian Science and Presbyterian services. Later in life, he was quoted as saying, "My religion is to pay my obligations and keep my word."

By the time George was nineteen, he secured a bank loan and bought the drugstore from his uncle. He had also studied and became a licensed pharmacologist after lying about his age. Young George was able to buy a second pharmacy from his profits, and he became a certified optometrist. It wasn't uncommon for someone to study and become licensed himself, because doctors were expensive and social security did not yet exist. He fell in love with his customer and neighbor Lillian Kraus, and the two soon had a daughter named Romola. George was barely in his twenties, but had a strong sense of responsibility. He was running two drugstores, providing services as an unlicensed doctor, writing prescriptions for glasses, raising a family and studying law at night.

When George was twenty-four, he opened his own law practice. He became a prominent divorce lawyer but specialized in criminal law and represented several Chicago labor unions. He spent much of his time defending the dark side of humanity, including those who committed crimes that he would later commit himself. Remus hired a legal secretary named Imogene Holmes. Imogene was part of a wealthy family, telling George that she came "from the top drawer." George and Imogene had an affair that eventually led to the end of his first marriage. Remus divorced Lillian in 1917, but maintained a good relationship with her and their daughter Romola, who got along exceptionally well with her father.

When Prohibition hit Chicago in 1918, many bootleggers turned to Remus, whom they trusted, for legal representation. Underworld figures regularly visited Remus's office at 167 North Clark Street, setting him on the beginning of his dark path. Remus's dealings with members of organized crime were strictly business. He knew Al Capone only vaguely through his business dealings. As a criminal defense lawyer, he witnessed several of his clients executed in the electric chair. It was because of his attendance at these horrific events that he came out strongly against the death penalty. His advanced knowledge as a lawyer and pharmacist was the perfect concoction to aid his ambitious rise to wealth and power. If the perfect candidate to become a bootlegger ever existed, Remus was it. His rationale was that if gangsters of limited intelligence could make money bootlegging, then surely he could do better. George sold his law practice and moved with Imogene to Cincinnati.

Relocating to Cincinnati was a strategic and well-planned move since three-quarters of the country's bonded whiskey was within three hundred miles of the city. After Prohibition became law, millions of gallons of whiskey sat in government warehouses and distilleries. With the entire country dry, whiskey certificates were easily and cheaply had. Remus began buying them up and soon was the largest owner of distilleries in the United States.

Using his skills as an attorney, Remus found a loophole in the Volstead Act, the very law instituting Prohibition. It would make him millions. He would buy distilleries and pharmacies and use government-approved certificates to sell liquor to himself for medicinal purposes. He would then hire men to hijack the shipments of his own liquor, which Remus would sell for a profit. A very small amount ever hit the pharmacy shelves as medicinal whiskey. Each case contained three gallons. Remus paid as little as $0.65 per case to remove whiskey from various warehouses. It would then sell for $80.00 or more per case. The operation was meticulously planned and brought in large sums of cash daily. Within a few months of Prohibition taking effect, Remus had set up more than a dozen drug companies to sell the liquor to and was depositing as much as $15,000.00 per day into banks. When one of his drug companies had removed enough liquor to catch the attention of law enforcement, he would simply close that company and open another. As time passed, the financial success of the business grew, as well as its cost.

George Remus was running a bootlegging empire of epic proportions, and it wasn't cheap. At the height of his success, he had as many as three thousand well-paid and fiercely loyal employees on the payroll. They represented all walks of life, from the servants at his farm to many policemen and politicians. His bribery reached as far as the attorney general, whom he successfully bribed for $500,000. During one quarter in 1921, Remus deposited $2.7 million into one Cincinnati bank.

Remus was constantly seeking acceptance from the community in Cincinnati. He set out to accomplish this by buying a huge farm in Price Hill, the most affluent suburb at the time. The property at 825 Hermosa Avenue matched his legendary status, complete with a large, newly renovated mansion and several houses for his many servants, chauffeurs and their families. It also showcased fully landscaped gardens, a greenhouse, a carriage house and several racing thoroughbreds housed in a stable. In 1920, Remus spent roughly $750,000 to renovate and develop the land. In today's money, the project would cost several million dollars.

George and Imogene were married in June 1920, and began hosting extravagant and elaborate parties at their new home. The mansion was nicknamed "the Marble Palace." Guests visiting the mansion found many unique artifacts, such as statues and sculptures, a collection of rare books and paintings, a gold piano and an autograph from George Washington. The parties were legendary. Remus was known for slipping $100 bills underneath guests' dinner plates. The Remuses hosted a party on March 21, 1921,

The solarium room at the Remus mansion. *Courtesy Jack Doll Collection, Delhi Historical Society.*

to celebrate the completion of their new $100,000 Olympic-size indoor swimming pool where each guest received an engraved gold Elgin watch. On New Year's Eve 1922, the Remuses outdid themselves. The exclusive guest list boasted one hundred well-connected couples. As a parting gift, the following morning the men were presented with diamond watches, and the women each received a new automobile. Similar parties continued, including a night when a fifteen-piece orchestra serenaded guests while Imogene, who was a talented swimmer, made an appearance in a water ballet. George and Imogene were well on their way to gaining the acceptance that they so dearly longed for.

When Remus had bought his Price Hill mansion, he had also bought a property near Queen City Avenue called "Death Valley Farm." This allowed him to increase the size of his operations in a hidden corner of the city near Westwood. Business was booming, but many forces were trying to take down George and his empire. Remus had a fleet of fifteen unmarked canvas-topped trucks he used for transport, and many times he used fruit and vegetables to conceal the cases of liquor. He also employed several heavily armed men to follow and protect the shipments since many gangs were on the lookout to hijack liquor. His extremely successful venture relied heavily on the large amounts of bribe money he paid. He estimated that during his heyday, he had spent $20 million on bribes.

There were only two men in the world, it seemed, that Remus could not bribe. They were the Prohibition directors for the states of Indiana and Kentucky, and they had made a special trip to Cincinnati to secretly raid Death Valley Farm. Through his large network of contacts throughout the community, George had heard that two strange men, possibly Prohibition agents, were in town. Early on that Sunday morning, Remus had sent a messenger from his Price Hill mansion down to Death Valley Farm to collect some money. He told the messenger to be sure to tell the men to clear out all of the liquor. The messenger collected the money but forgot to relay the message. Only hours later, the agents performed a raid on the farm. Remus and twelve of his men were charged and found guilty. Remus was sentenced to two years in jail and a $10,000 fine. For the first time all of the planning had failed. When Remus and his twelve associates departed Cincinnati for an Atlanta jail, they did it in style. Remus hired a special luxury train car that was attached to a regular train. Imogene accompanied her husband and the men on the trip while they enjoyed yet another party, with a private chef cooking gourmet meals.

While in jail, Remus continued to use his power to his advantage. He did his time in a separate building away from the general prison population called "Millionaire's Row," which was a small apartment with a private bathroom and kitchen. He had fresh flowers delivered daily. Imogene visited frequently, cooking and cleaning for George and sometimes spending the night. She had also made arrangements for George to make his time easier. For $1,000 per month, he was able to make unlimited phone calls, go outside of the jail on shopping trips and occasionally take Imogene out on the town in Atlanta, where they would spend the night in a hotel.

While in Atlanta, a friend of Remus told him of a very powerful and persuasive Prohibition agent named Franklin Dodge. With a successful bribe, Dodge had the power to possibly grant both of them a pardon. George sent Imogene to feel him out, telling her to get close to him and see what he was capable of. As she moved in and worked to bribe Dodge, she quickly fell in love with him. He was a notorious womanizer. Imogene had fallen deeply in love with one of the men whose job was to take down men like George. Imogene and Dodge began working together to strip Remus of his fortune. This proved an easy task since

Imogene was left with power of attorney during George's time in prison. The two systematically plotted Remus's demise. Soon after starting their affair, Dodge quit his job with the Justice Department and moved into George's Price Hill mansion. He used Remus's personal items such as hats and cufflinks and slept in his bed. Imogene and Dodge also traveled frequently, often staying in a hotel as a married couple under an assumed name. Imogene gave Dodge $100,000 worth of George's jewelry. She also sold one of George's largest distilleries at a deep discount of $81,000 and sent him a check for $100 as his share. The two lovers even engaged in intimate acts in the warden's office, only one hundred yards from where George was locked up. They filed papers alleging that George was an illegal alien because his father was never naturalized to try to get him deported. Remus sat in jail, deeply disturbed by the reports of dealings between Dodge and his wife.

Imogene had made up her mind that she wanted her husband to be locked up for as long as possible. When Remus was discharged from Atlanta, he faced an additional incarceration period of one year. Dodge had been one of the men responsible for Remus's additional jail time, which he served in Troy, Ohio. Dodge sold a large portion of the whiskey permits that belonged to George and kept the money. He had even registered one of George's cars in his own name, taken it to his hometown of Lansing, Michigan, and changed the plates. Imogene ranted to her family how she would somehow "take care of George," even if it meant killing him. At the Troy jail, Remus was treated as a regular inmate for the first time. Upon hearing news of Imogene and Dodge's deceitful actions, Remus had fits of rage inside his cell, breaking furniture and sobbing uncontrollably. He could not stand the thought of his wife and Dodge together. His empire, fortune and sanity were slowly melting away as he sat helplessly in his cell.

Each day George grew more despondent, having been thrust into a deeply depressed state. Finally the day of his release came. On April 26, 1927, George Remus was released from the Troy jail at midnight. He was driven home by his longtime friend, George Conners. Remus was looking forward to some relaxing back at home, far away from a jail cell. The two arrived at Remus's Price Hill mansion about 4:00 a.m. What the two men found shocked them. All of the doors and windows were nailed shut, and George's clothes were on the ground outside the back door. The men had to enter through a window into the mansion. An even more disparaging scene awaited them inside. All that remained of the mansion was a table, a few chairs, a gas range and sixty-three pairs of Imogene's shoes. In his bedroom, Remus found a cot and a pair of men's shoes that did not fit him. Imogene had stripped the mansion. There were no furnishings, chandeliers, paintings or sculptures. Imogene even had stonework removed from around the pool and sold. She had even taken Remus's prized signed portrait of George Washington, his rare books and his equally rare collection of Washington letters. At the sight of the bare mansion, Remus fell to his knees and wept.

Shortly after his return home, Remus learned that his life was in danger from a reporter for the *St. Louis Post Dispatch*. Franklin Dodge had contacted some members of a gang in St. Louis called the Regan Rats and promised $15,000 if they would kill Remus. After learning of the news, Remus applied for and was granted a permit to carry a gun. At an Indianapolis railroad station George Conners spotted the gang and convinced Remus to catch the next train. Later it was learned that the gang intended on taking the train, staging a fight with Remus and killing him. It was also revealed that a contract had been taken out on George Conners's life.

Fearing for his life, Remus became obsessed with his safety and would wander the grounds surrounding the mansion looking for imaginary men with a flashlight. He also told Conners that he would see hallucinations of Imogene and Dodge together. Eventually Remus and Conners moved out of the Price Hill mansion and into a suite at the Sinton hotel in downtown Cincinnati. Imogene continued ahead with the divorce, and Remus's rage and despondency deepened. He went so far as attempting to throw Imogene's lawyer out of a window during a deposition. The day before their divorce hearing, George received information that Imogene and her daughter Ruth were staying at the Alms Hotel in Walnut Hills. He waited outside for the two all day without success. Later that night, Remus had dinner with Conners, his driver George Klug and his secretary Blanche Watson. Remus then had Conners take him back to his Price Hill mansion to spend the night before the proceedings the following day. It would be the last time he would ever return to his once-prized estate.

The next day was Thursday, October 6, 1927. George and Imogene were due in the Hamilton County Domestic Relations Court that morning at 9:00 a.m. George Klug arrived at the mansion at 7:00 a.m. to drive Remus to the courthouse. Court records show that Remus asked Klug to first drive him to the Alms Hotel stating, "There is something I want to discuss with her before we go before the judge." On Victory Parkway, near the hotel, Remus spotted Imogene and Ruth entering a taxicab and

Ruth Remus, daughter of Imogene. *Courtesy Jack Doll Collection, Delhi Historical Society.*

told Klug to catch the cab. Imogene spotted George and told her driver to hurry. Klug made a U-turn and a wild chase ensued. The chase crossed McMillan Street and continued toward Eden Park. Remus's car forced the cab to the curb near the greenhouses in the park; he jumped out and began walking towards the cab screaming obscenities. Imogene then told the driver to go, and the cab sped away once again. The large car with Remus in the back overtook the cab again about one hundred feet north of the reservoir. Imogene's daughter Ruth later testified that George pulled Imogene from the cab violently, shouting as he dragged her away. Imogene exclaimed, "For God's sake don't do it!" Ruth was close behind,

Imogene Remus, who was murdered in Eden Park. *Courtesy Jack Doll Collection, Delhi Historical Society.*

yelling, "Daddy, what are you going to do?" Imogene screamed for help from the cab driver: "Steve, for God's sake come help me!" She then ran back toward the cab. Remus went into a wild tirade, spouting profanities at Imogene as he caught her. The peaceful morning silence was broken as he held a gun to her abdomen and pulled the trigger. Imogene fell into the cab but quickly jumped back out the other side as Remus continued his pursuit. She ran away with her hands in the air screaming, "Won't somebody save me–won't somebody save me?"

An automobile stopped and picked up Imogene, taking her to the hospital. Remus gave up his pursuit and threw his gun away as he ran out of the park. The gun was not found until years later when a child recovered it during an Easter egg hunt. Remus walked down Gilbert Avenue, where a driver offered him a ride. He was taken to the railroad station, where he then took a cab to city hall. Only thirty minutes after he shot Imogene, George Remus walked into the police station at city hall and surrendered.

The couple was scheduled to meet with Judge Dixon that morning. As he waited in his chambers, Imogene was fighting for her life. After an unsuccessful emergency surgery at Bethesda Hospital, Imogene was pronounced dead at 10:45 a.m. An autopsy revealed that the bullet entered her body just below the ribs. It then passed through the stomach, liver, diaphragm, spleen and left lung before lodging just under the skin on her back.

In the Hamilton County Jail, Remus received the special treatment to which he had become accustomed. He was given an extra cell to use as an office, had twenty suits with him to keep his appearance up, was allowed unlimited visitors and was even given liquor. The charge brought against Remus was first-degree murder. He faced the death penalty, a penalty he adamantly opposed but so willingly and coldheartedly bestowed upon his wife Imogene. Shortly before his trial was to begin, the bootlegger turned murderer decided that he would defend himself. He would plead not guilty by reason of insanity, a novel approach at that time. During the trial, he would claim that the terrible things done to him by his wife and her new lover, for more than two years, had systematically caused him to become insane. One of the prosecutors in the case was Charles Phelps Taft, who as mentioned in an earlier chapter resided in what is now the Taft Museum of Art.

The murder and ensuing trial captured the attention of the nation and shared headlines with Charles Lindbergh's trip across the Atlantic. In the courtroom, Remus made jokes and was lighthearted. He had the benefit of being both popular and feared. He portrayed Imogene and Franklin Dodge as cold, self-involved characters who carefully calculated the takeover of his fortune and eventually his sanity. The jury was given the case on December 20. They reached their verdict in just two minutes, using a single ballot. After informing the judge that they had reached a verdict, the jury stayed out another three hours while enjoying a long lunch. When they reconvened, the jury foreman gave the verdict. The jury found Remus not guilty by reason of insanity. The *Cincinnati Enquirer* noted that the crowd in the courtroom cheered, and Remus shouted out, "That's American justice!" Imogene's family was appalled. A juror later said, "We felt, let's go out and give him a Christmas present. He has been persecuted long enough."

Remus was not guilty of murder but was not yet a free man. That night he hosted a party in his cell suite. His daughter Romola, a close circle of friends and two of the jurors celebrated with him. Remus was soon sent to a Lima insane asylum. Having lost, prosecutor Charles Phelps Taft worked tirelessly to have Remus committed to an insane asylum for life; however, the state's whole murder case had centered on the fact that Remus was in fact sane.

The gazebo where Imogene, the black widow, has been seen. *Authors' collection.*

Since the state's stance was that Remus was perfectly sane, he could not be confined to an insane asylum. He was eventually released from custody for good in June 1928.

After being acquitted and released, Remus attempted to get back into the bootlegging business but found that it had been taken over by violent gangsters. He spent much of his time in Florida and later had a modest home in Covington, Kentucky, where he died in 1952.

In Eden Park, many people have seen a woman in a black dress in and around the gazebo near the mirror lake. When Imogene was gunned down, she was dressed in all black for her divorce date. She was wearing a black silk dress, black stockings and a black hat from Paris. Paranormal investigators have spent massive amounts of money and time trying to capture a glimpse of Imogene's ghost. Some people experience cold spots or capture balls of energy on film in the gazebo. Others have reported seeing an apparition of Imogene in her black silk dress during early morning jogs. We have experienced her presence on more than one occasion. Her ghost seems to quietly roam the area and is quite curious about her visitors.

After living a lavish lifestyle, Imogene now resides in the beautiful park in which she lost her life. Her ghost seems content, seen by some gazing out of the gazebo onto the mirror lake. Shortly before George Remus went away to serve his term in Atlanta, he secured millions of dollars with friends and family and gave Imogene nearly his entire diamond collection, keeping just one for himself. The diamonds were never recovered. If you encounter Imogene's ghost, be sure to ask her where the diamonds are.

HAUNTING ACTIVITY SCALE
Frequency*
Intensity**
Type: apparition

BOBBY MACKEY'S SPIRIT WORLD

Just across the Ohio River in Wilder, Kentucky, sits Bobby Mackey's Music World. It is regarded by many as the most haunted location in the Cincinnati Tri-State area. Nestled near the Licking River, the building exudes a sense of dread, and for good reason. Bobby Mackey's is home to several ghosts from different time periods, and visitors sometimes experience more than a cold drink or a musical performance. The grounds of the club are forever linked with some of the most notorious characters and unsavory events the area has ever seen. Over time, the club has become extremely popular on the ghost hunting circuit and has been billed as the most haunted nightclub in America.

From the beginning, the site was a place where death was common. For more than forty years during the nineteenth century, a slaughterhouse stood on the site. The only remaining piece of the original slaughterhouse can be found in the basement. It is a man-made well that was used to drain blood and refuse from the animals on the killing floor. Animal remains have been found deep inside the well in recent years by employees. Several attempts have been made to fill in and cover up the well. The ominous hole, however, commonly referred to as the "portal to hell," will not be contained. It's as if the spirits within need to keep this connection open to our world. The well is a small opening with a much larger link to the club's disturbing past.

The well itself is linked through legend with the most notorious northern Kentucky murder of the nineteenth century. On February 1, 1896, a headless

Warning sign to patrons at the entrance of the club. *Courtesy Bobby Mackey's Music World.*

corpse was found about two miles from the site of the slaughterhouse in Fort Thomas, Kentucky. The body was dumped on a farm and appeared to have been thrown down violently in the spot where it lay. The corset had been torn open during the struggle. The victim's throat was slashed open widely. As the girl's lifeblood poured from her body, she fought her assailant, as witnessed by cuts on her left hand that lay open to the bone. The head was then severed with a dull knife just below the fifth vertebrae. Because of the large amount of blood on the undersides of the leaves at the scene, the coroner concluded that the victim was alive during the beheading. The job was not easy and the cut was not clean, changing directions several times as the killer hit bones.

By the time police arrived on the scene, hundreds of people had trampled the area around the body. Morbid curiosity seekers took items from the crime scene such as bloody leaves and tree branches. Some even tore small pieces of the girl's bloody clothing off to keep as souvenirs. The entire Cincinnati area was appalled, and the murder soon made national headlines. The story of a decapitated young woman was so shocking that many major papers around the country asked for a complete account of every detail with no limit on the number of words used.

After the body was found, it was taken to Epply's morgue in Newport. A large crowd gathered outside, and anyone who had any knowledge of a missing person was allowed to view the corpse. Without a head, the identity of the victim remained unknown. The woman was eventually identified by her shoes. On the bottom of the soles was the imprint "Louis & Hays, Greencastle, Ind., 22-11.62,458." The number on the shoe indicated that they were size three. The sales record was traced back to a young woman named Pearl Bryan. Pearl was a twenty-two-year-old woman from Greencastle, Indiana. She had told her family that she was traveling to Indianapolis and hadn't been heard from since January 28. When Pearl's brother Fred sent a telegram to her friends in Indianapolis, they responded that she had not been there. The family began to panic.

Police brought the victim's clothing to the Bryan home for identification. Authorities were unsure that the dress belonged to Pearl, because she came from a wealthy family and the dress was not of high standard. It was light blue and white with small checkered patterns. Through long episodes of sobbing, Pearl's mother told the police that the dress was one that was made over for Pearl out of one that belonged to her dead sister. Pearl's family held on to hope through the thought that perhaps Pearl had given her clothes to another girl. When police described the strange webbing of the victim's feet, the family lost any hope they had left. The dead girl was their beloved Pearl.

Police issued an arrest warrant for Scott Jackson, Alonzo Walling and William Wood after uncovering a series of disturbing telegraphs. After being brought in for questioning, the men involved began painting a dark picture. Pearl had fallen in love with Scott Jackson, a dental student in Cincinnati. Pearl's cousin William Wood had introduced her to Jackson. The Bryan family was one of the most respected in Greencastle, and Pearl had many admirers. She was beautiful, well educated and had a very likeable personality. After some months of dating Jackson, Pearl confided to her cousin that she was pregnant. She would later realize as she lay dying that trusting her cousin was a mistake. Wood betrayed her and contacted Jackson immediately, who was infuriated by the news.

Jackson was a smooth-talking, charming young man, but he also had an extremely dark side. In his home state of New Jersey, he was widely known as a con man and generally regarded as an indecent person. Before moving to Indiana, Jackson had worked for the Pennsylvania Railroad in the accounts

Pearl Bryan. This is believed to be the only portrait she ever had taken. *Courtesy Don Prout.*

receivable department. His boss devised a plan for the two to steal some of the company checks, cash them and split the money. Jackson eventually dodged all charges after agreeing to testify against his former boss.

As the questioning in the murder investigation continued, the details became clearer. Jackson sent several telegrams to Wood describing different recipes of drugs and chemicals that would cause a miscarriage. These all failed. Jackson then wrote to Wood telling him to send Pearl to Cincinnati. He said he had all the arrangements in place for Pearl to have an abortion. While at dinner with Walling and several other dental students, Jackson openly inquired to the group as to what poison would kill a person the quickest. He was told that prussic acid was the quickest but that cocaine was the next deadliest. Cocaine was a legal substance and readily had, so Jackson purchased some at Koelble's drugstore. Pearl arrived in Cincinnati, where she stayed at the Indiana House on Fifth Street. On the night of the murder, Jackson and Bryan were seen in Wallingford's saloon. Jackson ordered a whiskey. He then drugged Bryan's sarsaparilla, and they left in a carriage. From the beginning, it was unclear whether Alonzo Walling was with the pair the night of the murder. During questioning, Chief Dietsch made an attempt to learn the location of the head by taking the killers to view the headless corpse. *The Headless Horror* states that Pearl's sister Mary Stanley made one last plea, "Mr. Jackson, I come to you and ask where is my sister's head. For the sake of my poor mother and for my sister and for my brother I beg of you to tell me where my sister's head is. It is my last chance and I want to send it home with the body. Won't you please tell me, I beg of you?" Both men calmly and coldly stated that they did not know where the head was.

Because of the attention paid to the murder, crowds flocked to the farm to see the spot where the awful crime was committed. The farm owner charged ten cents to view photographs he took of the crime scene. Pearl Bryan memorabilia was sold in stores and at roadside stands. After a trial, the two men were sentenced to death by hanging. On the morning of March 20, 1897, the two young men ate a hearty breakfast and were told to prepare for the end. According to an article in the *New York Times*, Jackson told Sheriff Plummer that he wanted to clear Walling of any connection to the crime. He sat down and wrote a telegram to the governor. It read: "Walling is not guilty of this crime. I am." The governor replied that he needed more details, but if Jackson made a confession on the scaffold, he would postpone Walling's execution until further notice. As the execution neared, twenty-one-year-old Walling trembled with fear. He told a turnkey, "Jackson can save my life if he will, but he won't. I have tried in every way to get him to do it, but he will not. He ought to save me." The mayor asked Walling one last time where the head was. Walling replied, "Mayor Rhinock, before God, whom I shall soon meet, I do not know. I will not lie now." Just before they walked the steps to the top of the gallows, Walling pointed at Jackson and said, "That man can save me if he will. I die an innocent man. I was not there when she was killed." Just before the execution, both men were asked if they had any final words. Twenty-eight-year-old Jackson replied calmly, "I have only this to say, that I am not guilty of the crime for which I am now compelled to pay the penalty of my life." Walling's hopes of being saved were gone. As Walling trembled with his eyes staring down, he was asked if he had any last words. He said, "Nothing, only that you are taking the life of an innocent man and I will call upon God to witness the truth of what I say." With that, the two men were prepared for death. The gallows dropped, and neither man died right away. Onlookers watched as the men slowly choked to death for eight minutes.

According to several newspapers, a skull was found near the farm in November 1900, but because of primitive science techniques, it could never be confirmed as belonging to Pearl. In Doug Hensley's book *Hell's Gate*, he claims that the two men were linked to the well by claims of satanic rituals performed near the well. Many people believe Pearl's head may have been dumped in the infamous well at Bobby Mackey's. Psychics who have visited Bobby Mackey's have reported seeing a headless woman, as well as men who resemble Jackson and Walling. Our personal belief is that the ghost of Pearl may be a tulpa, something that has been created by belief in the minds of many people. A tulpa can manifest as a physical or spiritual being through sheer thought and willpower alone. This phenomenon is very real, and experiencing it firsthand can be frighteningly similar to seeing a ghost.

The days of gambling, drinking and entertainment started when Buck Brady bought a building on the site of the old slaughterhouse called the Bluegrass Inn. He soon reopened an upscale restaurant and casino called the Primrose. Prohibition had recently ended, and the new club was a giant success. Patrons enjoyed music, fine food, drinking and nightly floor shows. At that time, a mob faction of the Cleveland Syndicate was running several casinos in the Newport area, including the nearby Beverly Hills Country Club. The Primrose was regarded by many as the finest casino and restaurant in the area and was taking business away from several other clubs run by the mob. The Cleveland Syndicate wanted in, and they weren't looking to become a partner. Red Masterson was an enforcer for the Syndicate. He was sent as muscle to persuade Brady to sell. The crime family began to vandalize the Primrose and intimidated Brady and his patrons in many ways. One especially grotesque form of harassment was "ding-donging", when men would enter the club and relieve themselves on the floor of the club right in front of patrons. This infuriated Brady, who was trying desperately to maintain a positive image of his club.

Brady had been harassed for years and knew it was only a matter of time before the mob took his club, either by deed or by fire. He decided to end the harassment by taking matters into his own hands. On August 5, 1946, Buck Brady waited in the dark outside the Merchants Club Casino in Newport. Masterson exited the building and climbed into his new Cadillac. Brady pursued him, catching up with the Cadillac a block later. The sound of gunfire rang out through the streets of Newport as several shots flew into the Cadillac. An injured Masterson jumped from his car and hid behind another parked car. Both cars were wrecked. Brady and his accomplices fled on foot and disappeared into the night. Masterson survived the shooting but refused to identify Brady as the gunman, saying that he would take care of it in his own way. The mob now made Buck Brady an offer he couldn't refuse. They proposed that he sell them the club and leave town forever or stay and be killed. He sold the club for less than market value and left town. His days running the club were over. To this day, the old safe that was used by Buck

Brady when he ran the Primrose still sits in what is now a storage room and reads "Built specially for E.A. Brady." He committed suicide in 1965 after fighting a terminal illness.

After the Cleveland mob took over, the building was renamed the Latin Quarter. The club now featured cabaret dancers putting on regular shows for the customers. Framed pictures of dancing ladies from the Latin Quarter days still adorn the wall next to the stage. One of the girls danced under the stage name of Johanna Jewel and was the daughter of the club's owner. During that time, a crooner named Robert Randall would come to play at the Latin Quarter on a regular basis. Johanna was enthralled by Randall. She fell deeply in love with the charming, handsome young man and became intimately involved with him. Johanna feared her father's reaction if he found out about her love affair with Randall. Her father was a well-connected man with ties to the mob. Whenever Randall was in town, the two lovers would meet in secret, spending time together on the banks of the Ohio River.

Soon after their relationship began, Johanna became pregnant with Randall's child. She was able to keep the secret through the first few months of her pregnancy. Having a slender figure, however, a lump soon began to grow in her belly. When her father found out, he was infuriated. No man was going to impregnate his daughter with a bastard child. Randall was soon found dead. Details are sketchy, but her father had someone pay Randall a visit deep in the night, ending his life.

Johanna was devastated. She mourned her lost love, experiencing intense feelings of depression and rage. She harbored feelings of hate toward her father for what he had done. Not long after Randall was found dead, she devised a plan to kill her father. She attempted to poison his drink but was unsuccessful. Her despair grew deeper with each passing day. One night she climbed up behind the stage, walked across the catwalk and entered the spotlight room. She sat there for awhile feeling extremely depressed, at times sobbing uncontrollably. During investigations on the property, the sounds of a woman sobbing have been captured from this room when no one is inside. She wrote a poem on the wall, an emotional outpouring of her love and betrayal. To this day, the poem exists in the nearly inaccessible room. Her depression turned to thoughts of suicide, and she became deeply withdrawn. She went to her dressing room and took her life with a poison drink. Through unbridled sadness and intense pain, she slowly died.

Her ghost is probably the most well known in the club today. Bobby Mackey even wrote a song about the ghost called "Johanna." People have reported

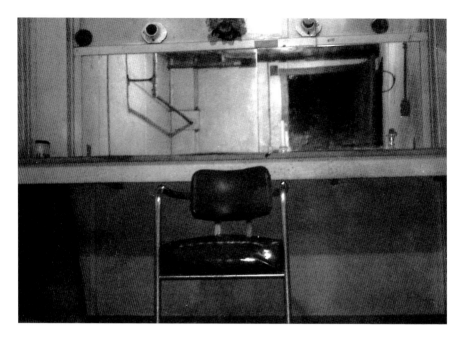

Johanna's dressing room, where she took her life. *Authors' collection.*

smelling her rose perfume throughout the club. We often have encountered her presence in her dressing room in the basement during our tours. On several different occasions we have heard footsteps coming toward us and stopping in front of us. We have captured things on film in this room, including green-colored orbs circling around our heads. We have also had questions answered on electronic devices used to communicate with spirits. Often orbs will be seen in the chair in front of her mirror. The mirror in this room does strange things indeed. We have several pictures where we have been standing in front of a mirror but have no reflections. When photographing this mirror, a demonic face has appeared in some of our pictures. It looks to be skeletal and has a clownlike appearance. We have also captured on film a shadow person watching us in the reflection of the mirror.

Over the years, there have been many stories of mob killings on the site. In the basement there are still bullet holes left from shootouts that occurred. The basement still holds many artifacts from the mob days, including a card table with a seemingly unfinished card game, moonshine bottles, bingo spinners and many more neglected treasures. There is also a staircase to nowhere, which acted as a trapdoor in case of a raid. This would drop down into the basement to make for a quick escape.

The Dark Side of the Queen City

The Latin Quarter used one of the rooms in the basement for interrogations, torture and murder. If someone was caught trying to cheat the casino, they were taken into the room and intimidated, beaten or worse. Hangings and shootings happened often in this room. Some patrons who were repeat offenders or became in debt to the mob were also given this special treatment. In order to dispose of bodies, the victims were given a "Newport Nightcoat," also known as a "Newport Nightgown." The victims were killed, their bodies were submerged in concrete and they were thrown into one of the nearby rivers. According to some local historians, if the bottom of the rivers were dredged today, many of these concrete crypts would be found.

One of the rooms of torture is known today as the "Room of Faces." If you take a black light down to the room you will see that the walls are still covered with dried blood. Sometimes the blood shows up in photographs, too. The stains have created many faces on one wall in particular, and some believe that these are the faces of the people who have died in this room. It is highly active with ghosts who do not seem to be happy. Any attempt to move things in the room will usually stir up spirits. A cabinet was moved in an attempt to clean this room and a water pipe burst immediately after. On other occasions a meter has spun around violently, and the lights will flicker. These spirits have been known to be violent as well. On more than one occasion, people have been scratched, bruised and injured. These are evil spirits that can indeed do you harm.

The building sat vacant until the 1970s, when a bar named the Hard Rock Café (no relation to the famous chain of the same name) was opened. It was a rough bar shared by two rival bike gangs: the Iron Horse Motorcycle Club and the Seventh Sons. There were large group fights and several fatal shootings on the premises. Finally, the police shut down the bar about 1977 because it was a public nuisance. The building was vacant once more, until someone would come to bring this club life instead of so much death.

Today the site is known as Bobby Mackey's Music World. For his entire life, Bobby Mackey has worked immensely hard, dedicating all of his efforts to doing what he loves most: performing country music. In the fall of 1966, Mackey boarded a train from Maysville, Kentucky, heading for Newport. He had a suitcase in one hand, his guitar in the other and seventy-five dollars in his pocket. He was on his way to begin work on the railroad. On the way, he passed over the Short Way Bridge. Through the rain and blowing trees, he saw the old Latin Quarter sitting near the banks of the Licking River. Mackey felt drawn to it from the first time he saw it. For a time, he regularly rode a bus that passed the building. He remembers the way the floodlights

Bobby Mackey's (at left) on the banks of the Licking River. *Courtesy Bobby Mackey's Music World.*

looked on the building, saying, "I could just see the people in there partying and having a good time."

Mackey worked on the railroad until 1970. In the fall of that year, he joined the band Red Jenkins and the Country Lads. Mackey loved old-fashioned country music from the time when he was a child. As a young man, Hank Williams Sr. was the first voice he recognized. For years, he played clubs like the Apple in Woodlawn, the Chuck Inn and the Boulevard. According to Mackey, the next step in his career was the decision, "Either move to Nashville or get my own club." He bought the club on Licking Pike with his wife Janet and partners Jean and Norman Stamper, and within ten years he was the sole owner. The music he plays bridges a connection with people and their emotions, such as his song "Hero Daddy," which went to number one in Cincinnati. Today he is a well-respected member of the community as a singer and business owner.

Many people across the globe believe Mackey's club is haunted. After more than thirty years in the club, is Mackey a believer? "No," he says, "I don't believe in that type of thing. It can't be proved or disproved." When asked about his take on the believers, he simply offers, "Maybe they know something I don't." The resident spirits at the club are probably on Mackey's side. "I've had a lot of good luck through the years," says Mackey. When visiting today, patrons can expect the same things that Bobby Mackey's has always had; good times, good company, bull rides and nightly performances by Bobby Mackey and the Big Mac Band. "I think people one hundred years from now will still talk about the place and how much fun they have had here," says Mackey. Many people come to the club hoping to catch a glimpse of a ghost but find themselves staying for Mackey's unique brand of country music.

The atmosphere of the basement is much more sinister than the dance floor above. As soon as the basement door is unlocked and thrust open, it is obvious why this place is known to be haunted. You can sense the death encompassing you, and the air is thick with the horrors that occurred here. These lost souls do not take kindly to visitors and can react very violently. We have encountered spirits on nearly every visit to Bobby Mackey's Music World. This place is full of spirits that mean no harm, and those who loathe the living. On one occasion, we picked up a disturbing EVP (electromagnetic voice phenomenon) calling us "spirit stalker." Many voices have been heard on our voice recorder calling us names, taunting us, warning us and responding to questions. Provoking these spirits will get you physically injured. Full-bodied apparitions have been seen here. One of the more photographed ones is the shadow person who walks along the back wall, always from right

The stage inside the club. *Courtesy Bobby Mackey's Music World.*

to left, wearing what appears to be a cowboy hat. There are countless souls that reside in this basement. Upon leaving the establishment, it is common to leave with more than you bargained for. Some people leave with intense headaches while others become physically ill. Spirits have been known to follow you home, plague your dreams, play tricks on your mind and affect things like lights and faucets. The slogan at Bobby Mackey's is "The way it was is still the way it is." These words hold so much more meaning when talking about the haunting that occurs here. At Bobby Mackey's, you can always enjoy great country music, ride the bull and party with the ghosts.

HAUNTING ACTIVITY SCALE
Frequency***
Intensity***
Type: apparition, poltergeist, intelligent ghost, nonhuman ghost, residual imprint, shadow people, tulpa

MANIACAL MELODY

One of Cincinnati's most iconic buildings rises majestically above Elm Street, keeping watch over the city since the time when streetcars and canalboats passed through its shadows. The grand Victorian Gothic structure stands as a visual testament to the city's golden era; however, it is what lies beneath Music Hall that gives the building's façade a more mysterious and sinister appearance. To understand what haunts Music Hall, you must travel to the intersection of Twelfth Street and Central Avenue. This quiet and unassuming area on the northeast corner of the intersection holds an ominous connection to the city's past. Here stood the first public hospital in the United States. What patients experienced here, by today's standards, would be considered malpractice and torture.

In 1795, the population of Cincinnati was only five hundred. By 1820, the number had reached nearly ten thousand. The streets were overrun with the homeless and the mentally ill. Cincinnati Township was quickly finding out that its informal approach to disease and the welfare of its citizens was not suitable. On January 21, 1821, an act was passed in the legislature establishing a Commercial Hospital and Lunatic Asylum for the State of Ohio. The area was to be no less than four acres and located within one mile of the public landing on the Ohio River. The state donated $10,000 in depreciated bank bills to the project, of which only $3,500 was realized in actual funds. The act establishing the commercial hospital proclaimed that the trustees of Cincinnati Township were to provide the "safe keeping, comfort, and medical treatment of such idiots, lunatics, and insane persons of this state as might be brought to it for these purposes."

The "Commercial" in the hospital's name required the trustees to admit and care for, without charge, all boatmen belonging to boats owned by citizens of Ohio and all boatmen who were citizens of states that provided reciprocal care to boatmen of Ohio. The Miami Canal ran just outside of the hospital and behind the land that would later be home to Music Hall. Additionally, the trustees were required to receive and care for all paupers of Cincinnati Township free of charge. Costs were paid by the state, county or family depending on economic status and place of residence. All others were charged two dollars per week for board and medical treatment.

Daniel Drake, who founded the Ohio Medical College, is often credited with turning the idea of the hospital to reality. Drake himself drew the plans for the original building and was paid ten dollars by the township for this service. The Commercial Hospital and Lunatic Asylum operated in connection with the Ohio Medical College, and Drake used the facility as an opportunity to afford experience to his students. The faculty of the college would render free services to patients, and in return they were given access to the hospital for the purpose of observation of the treatment of diseases and surgical procedures.

Within months of opening its doors, the building was serving as a general hospital, insane asylum, orphan home, almshouse, medical college and distribution point for relief efforts. It was a three-story building with the first floor being cells for men, the second floor having accommodations for women and third floor holding a lecture hall for students. The hospital was completed in 1823 and had four floors, including a basement. The lunatic department was completed as a separate building in 1827. After subsequent additions in 1833, the hospital totaled 150 beds, with a maximum capacity of 250 patients.

Soon after opening its doors to the public, the hospital began to garner a bad reputation. By all accounts, the conditions were appalling. Visitors would become physically ill from the stench of filth, human waste and death. The lunatic department was especially unforgiving. Patients deemed mentally ill or otherwise not of sound mind were chained to the floor, where they would wail and scream day and night. There were so many deaths here that the superintendent was nicknamed "Absalom Death."

The hospital was a permanent home for many of the patients. There was no privacy. Patients of the facility experienced nothing less than a chamber of horror. Many treatments of the time are seen today as bizarre

Commercial Hospital and Lunatic Asylum. *Courtesy Don Prout.*

and sadistic rituals of torture. The practice of bloodletting was believed to treat many illnesses by purifying the blood. Doctors would drain blood from the arms, neck, temples or wrists. Primitive devices and leeches would be used to spill large amounts of blood, and sessions would usually stop only when the patient lost consciousness. It wasn't uncommon to have one patient emptied of hundreds of ounces of blood over several dozen sessions. The practice was often an intense battle, with patients having to be subdued and restrained as blood was spilled and thrown in all directions.

The sealed windows of the hospital held in the stench of human waste from overflowing chamber pots. The severe lack of physical activity caused chronic constipation in patients. In some cases, if a patient became uncontrollable, laxatives were given to create a calming effect by means of distraction. Other treatments included short periods of starvation, enemas, induced vomiting and extremely hot or cold baths. Some patients faced the tranquilizer chair and were held immobile in a sitting position for hours to lower their pulse and blood pressure. Others were placed on boards spinning at great speeds with their heads facing out, so as to force blood into the brain. Tranquilizers and narcotics such as morphine, various tonics, wine, ether, molasses and sassafras oil were used as patient control methods. Some accounts state that poison hemlock would be used on especially difficult patients, which would leave them temporarily paralyzed for days. When substances were either unavailable or insufficient, the staff would resort to forceful restraint or in some instances outright abuse in the name of treatment.

The hospital was responsible for taking in the city's poor and unwanted, and it was also responsible for their proper disposal when death came for them. Cincinnati Township appointed a plot of land as a potter's field to bury the city's poor, indigent, suicides and unknowns that is located under present-day Music Hall. Once the life of these souls ended, they were thrown into the ground like so many pieces of trash. Well-to-do citizens of Cincinnati Township did not afford them even the simplest luxury of a wooden box. Their bruised, battered and scarred bodies were simply dumped into the potter's field. No one knows just how deeply permeated the soil is with the forgotten bodies of the insane. Today the ground is soured with thousands of corpses forgotten by history and time. Those lost souls who disappeared from society still haunt the area today.

In the fall of 1832, Cincinnati was stricken with a cholera epidemic that would leave hundreds dead. The canal system was a source of commerce for the city, but it also brought disease. The stagnant water in the canal was the perfect breeding ground for cholera. Canal workers regularly died of the disease. Those stricken with cholera would suffer from extreme bouts of vomiting, diarrhea and cramps. Many children became orphans because of the epidemic. As a result, an orphan asylum was constructed on what is now the site of Music Hall, near the potter's field. By 1837, the Commercial Hospital was at capacity and began sending patients with infectious diseases to the orphan asylum. The orphanage then became known as the "Pest House." The city's resources were strained, and more tragedy was yet to come.

The year 1849 was especially tough for Cincinnatians. Another more serious cholera outbreak occurred. Many people died of dehydration only hours after showing the first symptoms. The treatment was nearly as torturous as the disease itself. Doctors prescribed calomel, a form of mercury chloride, for the treatment of cholera. Patients who were treated with this dangerous chemical would routinely lose their hair and teeth. Many patients died of mercury poisoning during treatment. Citizens fled to the community of Mount Pleasant to escape the grip of the deadly disease. After the epidemic had ended, residents changed the name of the community to Mount Healthy in honor of their good fortune. By the end of the 1849 cholera outbreak, over

Maps showing the Orphan Asylum and later the potter's field. *Courtesy Doolittle and Munson.*

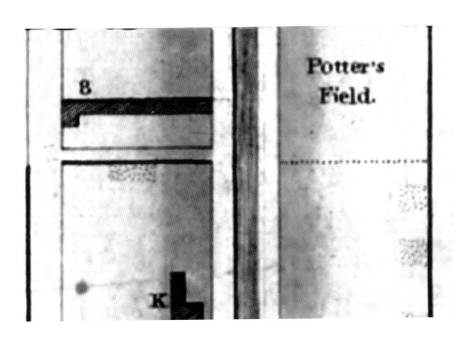

eight thousand Cincinnatians had succumbed to the disease. The ground used for the potter's field swelled with bodies.

The German population of the city held their Saengerfest, a choral festival, over the area of the potter's field as early as 1867. A tin-roofed wooden structure was erected by the Saengerbund Singing Society, at which time human skeletal remains were unearthed. Stories of transparent beings walking the land soon followed. One year, heavy rain pelted the tin roof loudly and relentlessly during the festivities, causing delays in the music. Reuben Springer, a prominent citizen, contributed a $125,000 challenge grant with private funds for the construction of Music Hall in what is believed to be the nation's first matching grant fund drive.

Once the plans were put into action to build Music Hall, the exhumation of countless bodies began. Many large dry goods boxes were found to be filled with scattered and mixed bones and broken and crushed skulls. Not a single full skeleton was found. Crowds began forming at the site, and without security guards there was no way to protect the site from theft. Skulls were prodded with fingers poking into empty eye sockets. Medical students stole bones and skulls during the night. The souls who finally found peace away from the confinement of the hospital were once again dishonored. Many bones were disinterred during the period from 1876 to 1879 and were relocated to Spring Grove Cemetery.

The original structure took only one year to complete, opening just before the May Festival in 1878. The wings of Art Hall and Exposition Hall were then added. With nearly four million red pressed bricks, the magnificent gem of the city was completed at a cost of $446,000. During renovations in 1927, seventy more grave sites were disturbed. The bones were carefully placed in a four-foot vault and lowered beneath the base of the elevator shaft, where they lay forgotten for over sixty years. During renovations in 1988, more than two hundred pounds of human bones were unearthed, including those from men, women and children. The harsh injustices enacted upon these people are hard to comprehend. Do the insane and mentally ill from another era still roam the area looking for help that they could never find in life? Many ghostly occurrences take place in and around Music Hall, from the lighthearted to the disturbing.

During performances, some patrons have reported seeing people in nineteenth-century clothing mingling in the crowds, only to disappear. Doors open and close by themselves, and escalators are turned on by an unseen force after they have been turned off for the night. Ghostly footsteps can be heard throughout the building when nobody is there. The sounds of laughter

The foyer inside Music Hall. *Courtesy John Wright.*

Music Hall is still a masterpiece after 130 years. *Courtesy Wholtone.*

and talking are heard by night watchmen. Perhaps they are ghosts of a time gone by who are forever linked to this place. Some of the occupants are not as happy to be there. Night guards have reported angry whispers filling the elevator late at night. Perhaps they are justly upset with the impudence of those who have stomped atop the hallowed ground for nearly two hundred years. Guards have heard the sound of bodies hitting the floor as if invisible inhabitants are jumping from the balconies. They hear the ghostly sounds of a music box playing near the elevator late in the evening after all others have gone, perhaps from the orphanage era. A beautiful, otherworldly singing voice has been heard throughout the building, and apparitions have been seen dancing in the ballroom. Staff members have reported that while opening the building in the morning, they have heard someone practicing the piano in the symphony hall, only to find that nobody of this world was there. While locking up for the evening, one employee walked into the ballroom and discovered that it was filled with people dancing in nineteenth-century dress. He was unaware of any event being held there that day. He contacted his superior to inquire about the party and was informed that they had no reservations for the room. The employee went back upstairs to sort the matter out and found the room to be dark and empty. Outside the building, cameras have captured orbs and full-bodied apparitions walking the grounds. There is no lack of ghostly presence at this site. It is unknown how many spirits are still lost in these symphonic corridors. While visiting here we have captured numerous orbs, shadow people and apparitions on film.

Whether haunted by a dark history or by time itself, Music Hall holds more than 130 years of forgotten secrets within its walls. The weary souls are eternally bound to a dark and unforgiving solitude. The ghosts that haunt here have found freedom from confinement—only in death. The cries of the maniacal are swallowed up and replaced by the joyful sounds of string instruments. They lived a desperate life filled with tears and loneliness, only to die and be disposed of without dignity. They still roam Music Hall looking for the help that they so desperately needed in life. The building now stands tall as a magnificent grave marker for all those who have been lost, with hopes that the dead may no longer be disturbed.

HAUNTING ACTIVITY SCALE
Frequency***
Intensity***
Type: shadow people, apparition, poltergeist, bleed-through, residual imprint

BIBLIOGRAPHY

BOOKS

Beam, Alex. *Gracefully Insane: The Rise and Fall of America's Premier Mental Hospital*. New York: PublicAffairs, 2003.

Behr, Edward. *Prohibition: Thirteen Years that Changed America*. New York: Arcade Publishing, 1996.

Cist, Charles. *Cincinnati in 1841: Its Early Annals and Future Prospects*. Charles Cist, 1841.

Clay, Henry. *The Papers of Henry Clay*. Lexington: University Press of Kentucky, 1992.

Cook, William. *King of the Bootleggers: A Biography of George Remus*. Jefferson, NC: McFarland & Company, Inc., Publishers, 2008.

Eifert, Virginia. *Delta Queen: The Story of a Steamboat*. New York: Dodd, Mead & Company, 1960.

Feldman, Jacqueline M., and Roxenne Smith. *Stranger than Fiction: When Our Minds Betray Us*. Arlington, VA: American Psychiatric Publishing, 1998.

Grace, Kevin, and Tom White. *Cincinnati Cemeteries: The Queen City Underground*. Charleston, SC: Arcadia Publishing, 2004.

Grauer, Anne L. *Bodies of Evidence: Reconstructing History Through Skeletal Analysis*. Hoboken, NJ: John Wiley and Sons, 1995.

Grob, Gerald N. *Mental Institutions in America: Social Policy to 1875*. Edison, NJ: Transaction Publishers, 2009.

Hensley, Douglas. *Hell's Gate: Terror at Bobby Mackey's Music World*. N.p.: B.J. Fitz & Company, 1993.

Hurd, Henry Mills, William Francis Drewry, Richard Dewey, Charles Winfield Pilgrim, George Adler Blumer and Thomas Joseph Workmann Burgess. *The Institutional Care of the Insane in the United States and Canada*. Baltimore, MD: Johns Hopkins University Press, 1916.

Jackson, Scott, and Alonzo Walling. *The Mysterious Murder of Pearl Bryan, or The Headless Horror*. N.p.: Barclay & Co., 1896.

Kachuba, John B. *Ghosthunting Ohio*. N.p.: Cincinnati, OH: Emmis Books, 2004.

Koenig, Harold George, Michael E. McCullough and David B. Larson. *Handbook of Religion and Health*. New York: Oxford University Press, 2001.

Ohio Federal Writers Project. *Cincinnati: A Guide to the Queen City and Its Neighbors*. Cincinnati, OH: The Wiesen-Hart Press, 1943.

Ohio General Assmebly. "Acts of the State of Ohio." Springfield, OH: General Assembly Ohio, 1870.

Rose, Linda, Patrick Rose and Gibson Yungblut. *Cincinnati Union Terminal: The Design and Construction of an Art Deco Masterpiece*. Cincinnati, OH: Cincinnati Railroad Club, Inc., 1999.

Singer, Allen J. *The Cincinnati Subway: History of Rapid Transit*. Charleston, SC: Arcadia Publishing, 2003.

————. *Stepping Out in Cincinnati: Queen City Entertainments 1900–1960*. Charleston, SC: Arcadia Publishing, 2005.

BIBLIOGRAPHY

Vallandigham, James. *A Life of Clement L. Vallandigham.* Ann Arbor, MI: Turnbull Brothers, 1872.

ARTICLES

Adair County (KY) News. "Pearl Bryan's Head." 1900.

WEBSITES

Bella Morte. "Spring Grove—Cincinnati, Ohio," http://www.bellamorte. net/Spring_Grove_CIN.html.

Bogan, Dallas. "History of Abolitionist Clement Vallandigham." USGenWeb Project. RootsWeb. http://www.rootsweb.ancestry.com/~ohwarren/ Bogan/bogan265.htm.

Cincinnati Museum Center at Union Terminal. http://www.cincymuseum. org.

College of Design, Architecture, Art and Planning. "The Taft Museum." http://www.daap.uc.edu/library/archcinci/1taftmuseum.html.

Dark Destinations. "Pearl Bryan's Murder." http://thecabinet.com/ darkdestinations/location.php?sub_id=dark_destinations&letter=p&loca tion_id=pearl_bryans_murder.

Findsen, Owen, and Cameron McWhirter. "Flood of '97." Cincinnati Enquirer. http://www.enquirer.com/flood_of_97/history3.html.

Forgotten Ohio. "Spring Grove Cemetery." http://www.forgottenoh.com/ SpringGrove/springgrove.html.

Greater Milford Area Historical Society. "John M. Pattison." http://www. milfordhistory.net/Pattison.html.

Grex. "A Brief History of Cincinnati." http://www.cyberspace.org/~omni/cin2.htm.

Johnson, Michelle. "The History of Cincinnati, Ohio." Associated Content. http://www.associatedcontent.com/article/1905352/the_history_of_cincinnati_ohio.html?cat=37.

Kelley, Stephen. "The Continuing Story of David Sinton." Brown Publishing Company Network. http://www.peoplesdefender.com/main.asp?SectionID=36&SubSectionID=360&ArticleID=128834&TM=36723.43.

Library of Congress. "American Memory." http://memory.loc.gov/ammem/index.html.

Lowe, Cliff. "The Life and Time of Chili Cincinnati Chili." http://www.inmamaskitchen.com/FOOD_IS_ART/cliff/chilarttwo.html.

Mecklenborg, Jake. "Cincinnati's Abandoned Subway." http://www.cincinnati-transit.net/subway.html.

Mitchell, M.T. "Vallandigham, the Notorious." http://home.mindspring.com/~mtmitchell/Vallandigham.html.

Neumeier, Franz. "History of the Delta Queen." Paddlewheel Steamboating Organization. http://www.steamboats.org.

New York Times. "Govt. Pattison is dead; Ohio now republican." June 19, 1906, http://query.nytimes.com/mem/archive-free/pdf?_r=2&res=9B0DE3DE1E3BE631A2575AC1A9609C946797D6CF.

Ohio History Central. "Cholera Epidemics." http://www.ohiohistorycentral.org/entry.php?rec=487.

Ohio History Central. "Cincinnati, Ohio." http://www.ohiohistorycentral.org/entry.php?rec=681&nm=Cincinnati-Ohio.

Osborne, Carol M. "Frank Duveneck & Elizabeth Boott Duveneck: An American Romance." Traditional Fine Art Online, Inc. http://www.tfaoi.com/aa/2aa/2aa572.htm.

R.I. Society for the Examination of Unusual Phenomena. "Bobby Mackey's Music World." http://www.riseupparanormal.com/paranormal_world/Paranormal_World_Articles/Bobby_Mackeys_Music_World.htm.

Society for the Preservation of Music Hall. "A Brief History of the Cincinnati Music Hall." http://www.soc-pres-music-hall.com/history1.htm.

Spring Grove Family. "The Spring Grove Family." http://www.springgrove.org.

Swon Libraries. "Greater Cincinnati Memory Project." http://www.cincinnatimemory.org.

Taft Museum of Art. "Museum History." http://www.taftmuseum.org/pages/museumhistory.php.

Taylor, Troy, and Dark Haven Entertainment. "The Murder of Pearl Bryan & the Ghosts of Bobby Mackey's Music World." http://www.prairieghosts.com/bobby.html.

Video Producers, Inc. "Bobby Mackey's Music World." http://www.hauntedhouses.com/states/ky/bobby_mackeys.cfm.

Ward, Maribeth. "Pearl Bryan Murder was 113 Years Ago." *Greencastle Banner*, February 2, 2009, http://www.bannergraphic.com/story/1498261.html.

Zimkus, Charlie. "The Death of Clement Vallandigham." Vimeo. http://www.vimeo.com/4745060.

INTERVIEWS

De-De Bailey, interviewed by Dan Smith, July 28, 2009.

Bobby Mackey, interviewed by Dan Smith, June 29, 2009.

ABOUT THE AUTHORS

DAN SMITH

Dan was born in Detroit in 1980. He moved to Cincinnati and became enthralled with the rich history that the city had to offer. He is currently working on a history degree from the University of Cincinnati. He enjoys spending time researching the lost stories and tragedies long forgotten by Cincinnatians. In 2008, he cofounded Cincinnati Tours, Inc. The company's signature tour is "Ghosts of the Queen City," which he developed from his passion for history and interest in the paranormal.

TERI CASPER

Teri is cofounder and owner/operator of Cincinnati Tours, Inc. She works as Casper, the friendly ghost tour guide for "Ghosts of the Queen City," a haunted tour of Cincinnati. Having been a skeptic for many years, Teri now believes in ghosts through her firsthand experiences. She is currently working on a degree from the University of Cincinnati.

Visit us at
www.historypress.net